seasons of verse

seasons of verse

An Anthology of Poetry
by Members of the
Harvard Institute
for Learning in Retirement

Harvard Institute for Learning in Retirement
Cambridge, Massachusetts

Seasons of Verse is a publication of the Harvard Institute for Learning in Retirement, Division of Continuing Education, Harvard University, 51 Brattle Street, Cambridge, Massachusetts 02138-3722.

ISBN 0-9664257-0-7

To the members of HILR—past, present, and future

Cover photo by Jeffry Pike, cover design by Nora Cameron, printed by Benjamin Franklin Smith Printers

Contents

Foreword

Seasons of Verse is a culmination of twenty years of creative writing at the Harvard Institute for Learning in Retirement, a volume of poetic reflections—sometimes simple, sometimes complex, and always affecting—on the vicissitudes of lives led over a major portion of the twentieth century. The authors are all members of HILR, who wrote and submitted their works to the biannual literary journal, the *Literary Supplement*, and to its modest mimeographed predecessors.

Some authors were experienced, published poets; others may have composed their first work of verse for this purpose; still others were members of writing classes at HILR where their skills were developed and projects reworked towards inclusion in the *Literary Supplement*. All felt encouraged by the community of HILR to extend their creative powers and to share the wealth of their life experiences in print. For HILR was founded on the premise of a lifelong commitment to learning and new inquiry, and poetry is but one of a host of subjects that nurture the intellectual spirit of the membership.

The poems here embrace the particular and the universal. Expressions of tenderness, rage, love, sorrow, loss, vitality, time and memory, they are tinged with humor and whimsy, gravity and nostalgia. They are personal and political, revealing and abstruse, intimate and detached. Some rollick, others meander, within structures both tight and free-form. Above all, they represent the spirit and vigor of a group of people who have discovered in retirement wisdom and a life of creativity in poetry. In this volume they celebrate their collective achievements, inviting their peers and successors in the rich and lively world of HILR to take up their pens and compose.

Leonie Gordon, Director
Harvard Institute for Learning
in Retirement

Introduction

The poems in this anthology document the history of an extraordinary era, from the world wars through the technological revolution at century's end. They reflect the evolution of poetic style in that expanse of time. Some poets remain firmly rooted in traditional structure. Others have moved comfortably into free verse. A few have ventured into the realm of prose poetry. All of the poems are comprehensible to the intelligent reader.

It is the subject matter and the treatment of it that distinguishes this collection. This is the work of older persons; no other group could have produced it. While loneliness, loss, and casualties of life and time will be found here, there is no evidence of self-pity. These poems draw on a reservoir of courage which seems to be there for the later years, and on the healing power of artistic creation.

A number of poems reflect the unending search for personal identity and a meaning to life. Others approach death and aging from a variety of perspectives, seldom sordid, sometimes wryly humorous. Loneliness has multiple facets: among them, the pleasures of self-imposed solitude; the reclamation of self after divorce; freedom gained from the empty nest. Intergenerational conflict is a recurring theme.

Romantic love seems to have given way largely to friendship and sublimated contentments. It is significant that belonging to HILR has aroused poetic declarations of love for an institution which has met important human needs, replacing lost friends and family and offering emotional and intellectual sustenance.

Reversing Wordsworth's gentle chiding that "Little we see in Nature that is ours," a heightened reverence for the natural world marks these poems. The nuclear arms race and war, as well as the hazards of smoking and drinking alcohol, are captured in powerful images of their impact on individual human lives.

There is consciousness of vanishing time. There are many Proustian touches, places and objects invoking memories of the past. Old and new are placed in juxtaposition. The contrast is best understood by those who have experienced so much of both.

Who are these poets, these people who began, or continue to write, in their later years? Their previous occupations were as varied as the structure of their verses. A sample of poets includes a social worker, a textbook editor, a librarian, a self-employed business woman, and former college professors of English, psychology, and physics. When asked what motivated them to write poetry, their responses were equally diverse:

"I write poems because I have to. It's like catching a bus—first, it is there and then it isn't there and you have to get on or else it's gone." (This from a social worker.) The English professor said, "I want to create something with some degree of aesthetic satisfaction. To give satisfaction a poem needs unity, coherence, emphasis and form." The editor saw it differently: "I want to hold on to life as it passes. I want to synthesize the very essence of life, but it all disappears before I can grasp it." Still another poet said, "I don't write my poems; they write me. A poem invades me sometimes and it has its own intentions, like an unborn child."

The poems in *Seasons of Verse* were selected from publications of the Harvard Institute for Learning in Retirement during the first twenty years of its existence (1977-1997). Those not included here may be read in the albums of HILR publications maintained at the Dunlop Library at 51 Brattle Street in Cambridge. Many of the authors are no longer living. They remain among the constituency of a vital group who reach out through their poems to make new friends of HILR members and all their readers.

Finally, we wish to acknowledge the special efforts of Bernice Rosenbaum in amassing the raw material from which we made selections; of Fran Vaughan, for her consummate editorial skills and faithful vigilance over the manuscript; and especially, of Leonie Gordon who ventured beyond the call of duty in the preparation of this book.

Anthology Committee

Margaret Haskell, Chair
Hélène Lyne
Frances McCormick
Dale Van Meter
Bernice Rosenbaum
Frances Downing Vaughan
Charles Vivian
Liberty Winter

Interrupt Me in Brookline, Massachusetts

Frances Addelson

I wouldn't mind being interrupted
on my daily walk along quiet streets,
the wind in my hair, on the way
to the dentist, the market or the park.

This is the time I wonder about the brave Victorian houses,
proud possessors of carved wood
yet lonely among the lean, modern ones.
I marvel too at the first growth in the gardens
where often a digging neighbor looks up
ready to talk lovingly of his earthy labor.

Nor would I mind intrusion
when I turn onto the great highway
resounding with clanging streetcars,
peopled with strange accents and manners
true to universal patterns of small commerce, family interplay
and all the other comings and goings of humankind.

Only let me not be overtaken
on a dreary day after a night of
raking decades' ashes of indecision,
anguish and too little courage.

Rather, let the rift come swiftly
while I'm still exploring, still pursuing,
still awed by the beauty of natural things,
savoring the enduring gems of poetry and still
trying to understand our history,
what's happening to us today
and where our children are going tomorrow.

Fall 1995

Underfoot
Jean Cassidy

What elements of wisdom
To the four winds flew
When Alexandria's vast
Libraries of scrolls
Were burnt and trodden
Underfoot by Caesar's crew.

That very skill the sculptor wrought
Upon the Isle of Melos
Two milleniums ago
Lies now upon the beach,
Long ground to dust
Lit by the full moon's glow
And we, unknowing all,
Are walking on the marble arms
Of Venus.

Spring 1992

The Show Must Go On
Jean Cassidy

Casting is done for the Family Play
By order of birth, not by choice.
A role assigned is never exchanged
For another; each has its own voice.

Once the house lights are dimmed the drama unfolds
And players may not leave the boards
Till the curtain comes down, the applause dies away,
And the orchestra plays the last chords.

So don your disguise, a suitable mask
For the part selected by shame,
And play it so well that no one will know
That your soul was a pawn in the game.

Spring 1993

The Doll

Jean Cassidy

She sits in a small red rocking chair
Under an attic window.
A large black fly motors up and down
The dusty panes of glass
But there is no way out.
She sits, linked to the chair by
Silken cobwebs, handiwork of a
Missing spinner.
Straw-yellow hair of various lengths,
Victim no more to little scissors.
She sits; lace ruffles—bedraggled,
Torn and limp—hang off one shoulder,
Give her a rakish air.
She sits, a faded courtesan,
Unbending in old age.
The single eye
A cynical observer of the
Occasional quest in trunks and boxes.

Spring 1993

Ogunquit Reverie

Charles E. Cook

High above the surf I watched
the ordered waves rolling to the shore.
Symmetric curving fronts carved by
the shoaling tug, equispaced from
crest to crest in response to
inexorable law.

(Is this my life,
ruled by fetch and
constant pull of day to days?)

Yet in the symmetry a variety
unexplained by moon and sun and
shelving strand. No crashing spray
against the rock the same. Never-
repeating patterns of windblown
tops and wavelets reveal a
wonder indescribable

(and the gentle breeze and
tug of you has made my life
curl and splash, explode
in unpredicted ways).

I am drawn to this place.
   I am drawn to you.

Spring 1991

Tennyson, Anyone?
(for Erek)
Charles E. Cook

My elephant at tennis
is amusing to observe:
he isn't very dainty—
oh so clumsy is his serve.
His forehand smash is feeble,
and it really makes me grin
to watch him lob and volley
with a wobbly backhand spin.
He likes to stand at baseline,
firm grip upon his racket,
to wave at every passing ball
and vainly try to whack it.
Then if he rushes to the net
on little tippy toes,
he always trips and stumbles
on his elongated nose.
So when I play my elephant
I'm gentle as a dove—
I let him have a handicap
and start at 'forty-love'.

Fall 1993

From a Priestess of Apollo to the Great Goddess
Pauline Cooke

Thus from the dark stillness of unchained mind,
From thought before thought was,
Came time and lust to know.

Nothing once known can then persist,
Nor give its grace to those
Who come to learn its name.

Why must I linger here beside a spring gone dry,
Whose trees, now dead, once gave cool shade,
Where all is parched and sere?
Yet I will stay.

The road that ran to those bleak gates is faint,
Mere crumbled dust, and none awaits
The pilgrim come to seek anew life's prize.
I wait.

A gnawing wind devours rock.
Here time itself will wear away
And leave me lone.

Fall 1989

Fayerweather Street
Pauline Cooke

Big barny houses dreaming in summer,
Garnished with plantings and brick walks,
Dormered and dreaming.

Dreaming of ice men and coal ash,
Porch swings, palm fans, iced tea and ice cream,
Dreaming, dreaming and waiting.

Waiting for families, for snow forts and ice skates,
For straw hats or mufflers, coal trucks or painters,
Dreaming, dreaming and waiting.

Waiting, waiting,
Waiting for families; once more to be lived in.
Waiting for children, play tents in the backyard.
Big barny houses waiting and dreaming.

Fall 1994

The Ride
Hope Corken

As I ride and I ride
In the shadowy dusk
The path through the woods
Fades away.

Above, the great owls
Give my little mare fright
And she quickens her pace
Till we race through the night

By the light of the moon
With her pale, shining disc
And the stars that peep out
One by one.

We rhythmically gallop
Across the wide field
Toward the beckoning light
Of the stable ahead.

Soft whinnies of welcome
Will greet my sweet mare
As she munches the hay
In her stall

While I to the house
Will have to return
And leave the quiet evening
Outside.

Spring 1981

A Treasure
Myra Juliet Cotton, Jr.

I was walking briskly down Cambridge Street the other evening. There was a "Miller's Court" presentation at Sanders Theatre on the medical ethics of the right to die—something I am deeply committed to. I wanted to get there early so I could get a good seat.

Two children, about ten years old, stopped me and wanted to show me their treasure, a beautiful butterfly. I began to make a few polite noises, and then took a good look at their faces. They were glowing with the joy of what was in the box, and filled with trust—and generosity—that I would get an equal pleasure in seeing it. It suddenly no longer mattered whether I got to Sanders Theatre in time. I entered this enchanted world and the "other" world fell away for those few minutes. We parted, and I resumed my fast pace. I looked back once, and the children had gathered another adult into their world.

Sara Teasdale's lines came back:

> "Children's faces, looking up—
> Holding wonder, like a cup."

Fall 1986

Sorrow
Louise Crelly

Time does not sorrow sweeten
Nor loss lessen. As Emily says,
Sorrow brings chill
That seasons cannot warm

The rose is black
And the swan drifts down to death

Fall 1992

Night in the City*
Susanne Dubroff

At dusk she's wearing
strands of pearls
against her chic gray dress.
Nightfall and she becomes
one of those socialites out of *Vogue*,
dripping with jewels, but truly elegant.
Forget the rest—
the thin black man, the girl
resting her orange head on his shoulder,
the grandma peering in the nearest ashcan. . . .
Tonight she's your enclave,
the bee's lily;
she'll show you elegance
that's more than elegance—
a kind of mercy,
a grace.

Spring 1994

Those Magnolias
Susanne Dubroff

Marjorie!   Micheline!   Martha!

The way   those magnolias
      open up   to the sun
gaudy and crimson   and we
did nothing   for them!

Fall 1995

* Reprinted from *You and I: Poems by Susanne Dubroff*
  (Kinsman Press, Franconia, New Hampshire 03850, 1984)

In Brookline Village*
Susanne Dubroff

The way the Swedes
       sit in the sun
averting suicide.

A small park
like a small fate:

      marigolds,
        red petunias
and the mad silences

      of wild, white roses.

Fall 1995

Eating Out
Susanne Dubroff

On Saturday we crave
the illusion
of community.
A restaurant will do.
I absorb it all,
as in Baudelaire's
Les Foules:
the family party,
the tête-à-tête,
the couple next to me
arguing about why his mother
never liked her.
It's something you'll never
understand. To you it's only
food. You'd rather we invite

* Reprinted from *You and I: Poems by Susanne Dubroff*
   (Kinsman Press, Franconia, New Hampshire 03580, 1994)

10

people to dinner, exchange
a few worn-out words,
or read a book
and go to bed.
And if you have a cold
as you do tonight,
even you get to realize
you're being a beast.
Still, I'm never sure
I'm not unfair as I
stare into your silence
like a trapped bear.

Spring 1996

The Gisors Road, Pontoise Snow*
Camille Pissarro
Susanne Dubroff

Because I have painted you
I know you,
I am allowed to come here,
to speak of you again—
your lingering snows,
the brown houses
against a tight-lipped sky,
and that woman
in the black jacket,
sweeping, sweeping
the leaves from last year's summer.
It is a picture
about the faithfulness
of mornings, the shyness
of cities.

Spring 1996

---

* Previously published in *Plainsong* (Western Kentucky University, Bowling Green,
Kentucky, and reprinted from *You and I: Poems by Susanne Dubroff* (Kinsman Press,
Franconia, New Hampshire 03580, 1994)

The Old Mill
Susanne Dubroff

They are always getting married—so young to be husband and wife.

The photographer is always taking pictures Sundays at the Old Mill,
the bride's mother in mauve, the father kissing the cloudy bride.

A man in a black suit carries a toddler in a blue sleeveless
dress. Arms dangling by her sides, she straddles his hip,
these two the last to leave the old, never-changing Mill.

Spring 1997

Two Questions, an Answer
Susanne Dubroff

Sing
out of the foolish,
self-inflicted solitude,
wound that grows,
bitter tree?

Dressed as a showgirl
or a tightrope walker,
changing clothes
in front of them,
would I be better off?

Sweetness of the meadow flower,
dawn's tall reed
of endurance, you tell me,
"This is as good
as it gets."

Spring 1997

Style
Dorothy Dunlop

Clothes today are meant to hide
The real figure that's inside.
They take a woman's torso
And try to make it more so.

What could be bolder
Than a huge padded shoulder?
They can no longer define
The normal waistline.

Shoes with sharp points
Will ruin your joints.
For my personal vanity
I'll wait the return of sanity.

Spring 1987

To Emma
Etta Endahl

New town—Boston:
New walls,
Thick with traffic,
New directions,
Often I was lost.
A million people,
Yet not one friend.
I struggled to stay abreast.
When she appeared,
A woman in our building
Small and frail in body,
Sharp, bright eyes,
Invited me to tea,
She opened doors,
Wide and broad, in depth
And intellect.
Concerts, lectures, plays, books,
Best of all, HILR.
More than these,
Her love broke down the walls,
Transcended Time,
Connected souls.

Spring 1991

Report from Everest*

Shirley Foster

From '78 to '85
you could see the body of a Mrs. Schmatz,
a woman who had reached the top of Everest
but couldn't make it down:
you could see her sitting in a sort of crouch
encased in ice
at twenty-seven thousand feet.

She is youngish, determined,
believing there is more to life
than her dull job,
the meals to cook, the cleaning.
She is exhilarated
and a little scared.
Her husband wishes her good luck,
kisses her goodbye.

She is somehow
separated from her party, or
with them still but knowing
she is colder, weaker,
suddenly distraught,
the downward trip
impossible for her to make.
The last of four,
she slips her ropes and glides.
She hardly feels the fall.

Fall 1988

---

* This poem, published in issue #12 of *Sandscript*, a magazine for poetry, won the Proxade Davis Award.

I Dream My Grandmother
Shirley Foster

Stout, in cotton housedress,
freckled arms across her breast,
my grandmother stands in summer

waiting for me and smiling.
Awake or sleeping,
I know she is dead.

Then I am dead I think, or dying.
I never dreamed of her before,
her loosely pinned-up faded hair,

the racket of her laugh,
her unconvincing anger,
the scent of lemon tea.

Spring 1992

Summing Up
Shirley Foster

Remembering how I turned here,
not there, never saw
the clover, early buds,
bypassed steel suspension bridges
while testing rope inventions
over chasms, I see the rationale
of being where I find myself
and nowhere else, who I am—
not someone else.

Fall 1992

Advice to the Lovelorn

Bob Gallant

Don't pine for the passionate words which entreat;
Sweet nothings are not necessarily sweet.

"Your eyes are like stars" won't enhance an embrace
Once one understands what stars look like in space.
They don't even twinkle; they're dull and they're cold;
And some show their age (they're ten billion years old).

"Your teeth are like pearls" is not apt to seduce
A person aware of how oysters produce
Their pearls. Pearls are sore spots the oyster protects;
Now how can that possibly stimulate sex?

"Your lips are like cherries—so sweet and so ripe"
On closer inspection is clearly pure tripe;
For, under the fruit of the cherry, there sits
The hard facts of life and, my friend, that's the pits!

Fall 1986

The Ballad of Bald Billy Bell

Bob Gallant

Every All Hallow's Eve, through the streets of Penzance
Stalks the spirit of Bald Billy Bell.
Ah, 'tis seldom a soul ventures forth on that night
When the Divil comes up out of Hell.

Billy Bell was a buccaneer sailing the Main
When the Spanish doubloon was in vogue;
And he raided and looted and murdered and such,
Like your average piratical rogue.

Billy paid a stiff price for his ill-gotten gains,
As was clear at a casual glance:
He was missing an eye and an ear and a leg
And his hair when he came to Penzance.

Though an eyepatch, a kerchief, a peg leg, and wig
Covered up what pirating had cost,
There was naught Bill could do to disguise what he'd gained
In exchange for the things he had lost.

For the burden Bill bore was a big bloated belly
Brought on by imbibing of beer
Bought by blowing the boodle he brought back as booty
From being a bold buccaneer.

Then, one All Hallow's Eve, when Bill pulled out his purse
From his pocket, he violently cursed;
Not a farthing was left of his loot from the Main,
And he still had this terrible thirst.

Through the night, damp with fog, Billy Bell stalked the streets,
Seeking someone with money to spare.
But all of them fled from the man with one eye
And one ear and one leg and no hair.

Then, the Divil appeared and He offered old Bill
All the beer he could drink by the keg.
In return, all He wanted from Bell was his patch,
And his kerchief, his wig, and his peg.

Well, Bell whipped off his kerchief, his patch, and his wig,
But the peg was too much for poor Bill.
Said he, "Divil, me belly's too big—I can't reach."
And the Divil replied, "Then *I* will!"

And, with that, He grabbed Bill Bell's peg leg and He pulled,
And the peg popped right out like a cork.
And the beer in Bill's belly poured out like a flood,
Washing Penzance clear over to York.

Now, if you be in Penzance next All Hallow's Eve,
And you're thinking of tapping a keg,
Just remember this Ballad of Bald Billy Bell
(and the divil who's pulling your leg).

Fall 1987

To Err Is Human . . .
Philip Gates

I spoke of God, and yes, I mocked.
My pious faithful friend was shocked.
"Your cynic's face is but a mask;
For His forgiveness I will ask."

"Thanks," I said, "have a good day."
Then I added—"By the way . . .
when you have Him on the line,
Tell Him, please, that He has mine."

Fall 1991

Lilies of the Valley
Isabella Hagelstein

Each May along the fence in our backyard
The delicate white bells appear as if by magic,
Wrapped against the chill of late sharp winds
In sturdy, folding capes of green.
The first bouquet of spring,
So simple, quaint and dainty to the eye,
Does not bend in graceful arcs
But stands erect. I bend to chance a scent
And find the perfume heavy, unexpected
In such tiny forms. Spring's statement
Is a paradox: its fruits
Are hardy, formed with vigor and
Determination. The eye is tricked
And I am caught in wonder.

Spring 1985

The Pains of Nature
Isabella Hagelstein

I curse and fume at inconvenience bred
Of days reorganized and spent indoors.
Nature's quirks now rile as plans are shed
And extended hours passed in tedious chores.
Through spattered panes I watch the slanted rain
Wind-driven cross the yard and torture pines.
Limbs heave in calisthenic curves. The pain
Of Nature spreads throughout in nasal whines.
The plague of March floods then chills within
And out. I suffer with the Shannon rose
Its jagged branch no splint can bear. Then chin
Raised high I smile and take a tolerant pose.
The pangs of prolonged labor I recognize
And know that Spring's delivery is the prize.

Fall 1985

A Safe Haven
Ted Halperin

The subway train sways as it rumbles through the tunnel,
Enfolding the riders, who in hypnotic trance
Rock back and forth, back and forth like robots.
Each person locked in unfathomable thoughts,
Waiting, waiting to escape from this trap of steel and wheels
As it thunders into alcoves of light and a safe haven.

Spring 1990

Boogie-Woogie
Nancy Harrrison

The white keys crash and the black keys quiver;
The notes start rumblin' and the keys all shiver;
The big black box shows that someone's playin'
Boogie-Woogie.

The bong-bong-bong of the bass beats steady
As the fast-flying fingers on the top make ready
For the fascinating rhythm that shows someone's playin'
Boogie-Woogie.

Hands hammer tabletops, toes pound the floor;
Rhythm runs hot as they yell for more.
Can't keep still, shows you know someone's playin'
Boogie-Woogie.

What is this mad, merry, metronomic stuff
That makes quiet humans turn tameless, tough, rough?
That smooth, solid, diabolic, pulsating pound . . .
Boogie-Woogie.

Fall 1987

My Seventieth Year
Margaret H. Haskell

Some thoughts recur
like waves eating the shore.
Is this my last spring?
Will I ever see that friend again,
Or will death's eenie-meenie-minie-moe
alight on him?
Well, better him than me.

I'd like to buy a hawthorn tree,
but it's years before they flower.
Would I ever see it bloom?
I'd like to buy a dog.
I always used to outlive the dogs,
but now he might outlive me.

My father and mother are fading photos.
One man I loved is hair in a locket.
It's the color of fallen leaves
and it still curls in damp weather.
Sometimes I sniff it.

Spring 1994

Images of My Mother
Margaret H. Haskell

Lashless china-blue eyes shadowed by her floppy hat,
a swan neck with three wrinkles like bracelets,
her beauty a margin of patterned sand
diminished by every wave.

Her laughter peals on seashell teeth;
her voice springs from sea caves
I shared with her when tides were time.

My mother smells like dried lavender sachets,
like linens bleached in the sun.
I could be her bloodhound.

She enters my room gliding;
the invisible book on her head is unshaken.
Her bosom could support a bowl of oatmeal.

She tests my fever with perfumed fingers
and builds our cabin with buttered toast.

Spring 1995

Lay Your Hand on the Grass— You Can Feel a Heart Beating
Margaret H. Haskell

Roseleaf over roseleaf,
over and under,
turning summer—
a bird blue as thunder
flying between,
leaving, and weaving the glittering green
into a pattern of time in between.

Meantimes, in between times,

the lean season, coming between
summer and summer—
the wind keening
an end to meaning,
a skull grinning
and snow spinning,

then a new beginning
and the green coming—

Spring 1995

For a Child Not Yet Twelve
Margaret H. Haskell

Poised immaculate on the single instant,
soon comes the downward plunge of your nature;
now
you are innocent as a statue,
engraved and golden forever.

Time's flood I would freeze,
as in art I would stretch the pinpoint moment
to infinity.

But to you this time is
a chrysalis quick to be ripped
or a treasure-hunt trail
where, breathless, you follow the clues
to your future self.

Like water, you rush through my clutching fingers
and run laughing ahead to the fall.

Fall 1995

If I Be WASPish,
Best Beware My Sting
Margaret H. Haskell

I come from a tight-fisted, lantern-jawed people.
Slender in youth,
though in age we resemble the full-bellied wasp.

Bees can sting only once;
we sting again and again.

---

* Previously published in *The Ebbing Tide* and winner of editor's award for poetic excellence
 (National Library of Poetry: Owings Mills, Maryland 21117, 1996)

Our purse-strings are tight as our lips.
And though sometimes we glitter with rhinestones,
our real jewels are kept in the safe.

Some sneer at our sag-bottomed suits,
at our chilly houses and left-over meals.
We respond with the Boston Freeze.

We will spend our *all* for education.
From generation to generation
we engender mad poets and sometimes a president.

Fall 1995

A Sea Grumble
Margaret H. Haskell

The sea grumbles, sucks pebbles,
spits out old boots and broken bottles;
Sargasso weed blows bubbles
on the riggish tide.

West winds smell like watermelon,
east winds like salt herring;
storms bring a stink of kelp.
The spinning stones are rearranged
from year to year.

Childlike, we peer in pools,
see small villages—
a snail laboring up a mountainside
with waving horns that prick the current.

At low tide, we perish like jellyfish,
become a stain of wetness on the sand.
High tide lifts us;
exultant, we swing on our buoys,
cry harshly in gulls' voices.

Spring 1996

Going, Going, Gone
Margaret H. Haskell

The year the apple trees forgot to bloom,
at first no one noticed.
Then people said,
"It happens sometimes"—
and spoke of the year that had no summer. . . .
But then they remembered the bullfrogs,
once so many, now not seen for years.

Then, "Where are our winters,
the deep snows that held us spellbound,
the curls of wood smoke from every chimney?"

"And why is our cancer rate growing
so much among young people?"

"And our carefully nurtured children,
scientifically raised,
we read all the right books;
why has the median IQ declined?"

"Why so many child suicides?"

An old man said,
"The earth takes her revenge.
She has been raped and plundered.
Now she is dying
and we die with her."

Spring 1997

Future Imperfect
Margaret H. Haskell

Red Sox fans dream an impossible dream;
Mallarmé expressed the inexpressible.
Thomas Wolfe named the nameless and inchoate.
I wish to mention the unmentionable:
may I be reprehensible
and never, never fit in—
may they never point with pride
and say I am typical of their group.
Let me be a rattling skeleton in their closet
who will jump out like a jack from a box.

Rebels assist the iceberg future
to break through the titanic present
while Lady Astor cries,
"I asked for ice, but this is too much."

Newsmen make gentle obstetricians,
bringing forth the future
as a pink and tremulous babe
who might be put away to die on a baby farm;
nor will editorials do it—
for yesterday's sins are today's fashions
and tomorrow's habits.

They wept when the pig shed burned,
but someone moved the pig's carcass
and smiled when he licked his hot fingers.
Will you please pass the roast pork?

Spring 1997

Sonnet to a Friend Who Made Three Million (on a Pinball Machine)
Thelma J. ("TeeJay") Henner

A bright metallic ball enclosed in glass
Whose random movements make men cry aloud
Slips through the precious slits into the pass
Bemoaned, bewailed, and cursed at by the crowd.

The lightning shocks be-ring the trilling bells
Like piercing telephones in dead of night;
The existential acts in cold white shells
Themselves proclaim success by neon light.

The ball is caught and pushed once more to move
In never-ending whirls of flashing pools;
It struggles to avoid the stagnant groove
And by magnetic magic captures fools

Who linger in the thought that they are free
And pull the plunger still unknowingly.

Spring 1993

Hidden
Mary L. Higgins

A hospital is not my choice
of residence, had I a voice.
But here I came just yesterday
some therapeutic time to stay.

People prodded, people pried,
never finding, though they tried,
the tiny, frightened me inside.

Spring 1990

Lines to a Long-Ago Dancing Partner

Elizabeth Jamison Hodges

In Harvard's Memorial Church
On its roll of World War II,
I suddenly found your name,
The first time that I knew.

And remembering your dances with me
In old time Brattle Hall,
I saw you charm young angels
At some celestial ball.

Spring 1985

In the Running

Elizabeth Jamison Hodges

My race is a losing marathon
Between what I would and do get done.
At any pause for breath I find
Myself another league behind,
Yet clutch this consolation prize:
I have not lacked for exercise.

Spring 1986

Wedding Moment
Elizabeth Jamison Hodges

"Speak now or ever
Hold thy peace."
The moment quivers
Till release,

And serpent-like
It holds tense sway,
As if to smite
The bride's bouquet.

Spring 1988

Wallpaper
Elizabeth Jamison Hodges

There's a vine to creep
And a willow to sweep
Across a purple pagoda,
While ancient steps fall
To a Chinese wall
And peony buds below.

But the willow won't sway
And people don't pray
Inside a paper pagoda,
And none can descend
The steps to the end
Or see printed petals grow.

Spring 1988

Realtor

Elizabeth Jamison Hodges

If you need
a roomy place,
let me find you
one in space.
I have stars
on my list
you may have over-
looked, so missed.
And if you can
afford to pay,
some choice lots
on Milky Way.
Go have a taste
where freedom sings
on one of Saturn's
outer rings.
There put fresh stardust
in your pocket.
And how commute?
Express, by rocket.

Spring 1992

Gossamer
Lisa Kuhmerker

Just as the spider sails without dread
Out through the air on his gossamer thread,
So do my thoughts fly
To your heart from mine,
Strung on a secret, invisible line.
With my own longing
I give them strength,
Push them and pull them
To span the great length,
Till shining and airborne
They come through the blue,
Ready to find their anchor in you.

Fall 1991

Star Flakes
(Divinely Proportioned Stellar Fractals)
Milton Landowne

From any star do greater stars
Encompass cosmic divinity?
Or are there far more lesser stars?
Both ways go to infinity.

So if for you a larger star
Grandly points and guides you,
Cherish too those smaller stars
Which nestle close beside you.

Spring 1993

32

Loneliness
John Lerch

Loneliness is glorious.
Fantasies seek sanctuary
In the core of solitude
—Silence, exile and cunning—
For armor against the world.
Singleness is revenge
And being solitary
Sharpens identity
Alone.

Loneliness is glorious.
Thinking is ever circular:
Ponder, mull and reflect.
Stir the pools of memory
Stimulate the joyous harmony.
Indulge total privacy.
Defend the inward pilgrimage,
An armed crusade, of sorts,
Alone.

Loneliness is glorious.
In glum cathedrals stir
Disbelief and despair.
Stark sessions of selfhood
Bittersweet reminiscences
Incandescent essences
—*Sunt lacrimae rerum*—
In flights of spirit, we ascend
Alone.

Loneliness is glorious.
Erect a spire of meaning
Fashion lives of artfulness
—Life has loveliness to sell—
Sigh with wistful ambiguity
—With rue my heart is laden
   For golden friends I had—
Hideaway in the warp of time
Alone.

Loneliness is glorious.
In landscapes of nostalgia
We travel, memory-bound,
The world around
To meet ourselves.
—*Là, tout n'est qu'ordre et beauté*
   Luxe, calme et volupté.
An odd élite, the loners, out-of-tune
Alone.

Fall 1987

Bref, c'est la Normandie
John Lerch

Normandy is butter glistening in old crockery; it is a savory seafood crêpe served for a dollar at a nondescript brasserie in Etretat. It is a chrestomathy of pungent cheeses. Normandy is strong apple cider, sometimes wickedly distilled into calvados which can propel you across the channel.

On carnival days, there may be a gaggle of old ladies, seemingly drawn by Daumier, leaning against the wall of the village lavoir and decked in conical lace caps. They uncannily detect an alien predatory presence and flee.

It is gray: leaden skies, squat granite churches, entire farm hamlets in shades of gray surpass the pervasive grisaille of Paris. And yet Normandy is green: bright racing green, the green of Kent, of Eire, of Oz (the Emerald City), all this greenery rolled into one. Normandy is still a hodge-podge of hedges and TV antennas which bring the farmers fiscal bulletins from their suspect and remote capital.

Spring 1991

Lyle
Margaret N. Lewis

Why did you smoke?

That young rebellion of your college years
still leaves me lonely. Where now is all our fun
of lazy Chinese lunches in the Square?
the fun of browsing in our favorite shops
or trying on new dresses in Touraine's?
Where now are all your Sunday morning sews?
Even the taxi man knew where I went.
We cut out patterns while we chattered or sang,
and mixed "Mikado" tunes with basting seams.
Your Sylvia lunched on strawberries and bread,
hot buttered French bread. Do you remember that?

O! Why did you smoke?

You loved the world! You worked in many lands;
seeking ancient Egypt's tissue types,
or lineage blood groups of our Indians.
You cherished language, and from you I learned
to share a deep respect for living words.
Your clarinets had fallen silent until
your young friend brought their notes to life again.
Her father's party was your last affair.
You came, bald-headed, in your crimson silk.

O Lyle! Why did you smoke?

When they filled your room with music that last night
could you still hear the glory of the "Ninth"?
Gene slept near by you on the floor to give
you morphine when you whimpered in your pain.
New Year's Day! The nurse came back to help
us ease the drowning gurgle in your lungs.
While evening dusk returned I held your hand.
At last I spoke, "I cannot hear her breath."
"She's gone," was all the nurse could say.

O Lyle! Lyle! Why did you smoke?

Spring 1987

It's March!
Margaret N. Lewis

Toddlers tumble on
white-shrouded earth in snowsuits
bright as Easter eggs.

Spring 1987

Complementarity
Margaret N. Lewis

Dawn colors the hills on the distant shore and there,
Opal and polished steel, the waking bay
Spreads wide, now blooming rose and lupin where
Cloud reflections of summer sunrise play.

Over mussels and rocks and floating weed,
The morning tide creeps in as quiet as time.
Rock-fast, the feather-footed barnacles feed
As rising waters above their cirri climb.

Nearby the great blue heron comes to brood
On his accustomed rocks, as I on mine,
Enough companion for my solitude.
Can mutually exclusive needs combine?
Can I have this, yet many minds to meet?
This peace, yet share the city's urgent beat?

Spring 1994

Time
Margaret N. Lewis

Time isn't very long, you know,
Just twenty billion years, or so.   = 15×10^9
For every day since time began,   = 3.7×10^2 x1.5×10^{10}
Save half a dollar (if you can).   = $\$5 \times 10^{-1}$
You wouldn't have enough as yet   = $\$3 \times 10^{12}$
To pay off all our national debt.   = $\$5 \times 10^{12}$

Spring 1994

October Wine
Margaret N. Lewis

As the amber gates of evening close,
the yielding sun ignites the air,
throws golden light on golden boughs,
and crowns the wine-red trees with fire.

Can swelling grapes of summer days
produce a vintage that excels
the wine that touches not lips but eyes
with flaming trees on autumn hills?

Fall 1994

The Great Catalpa Tree
Margaret N. Lewis

Your massive trunk, your crooked boughs
       Trail shadows of white lace
From multitudes of clustered blooms
       High in your green embrace,
As once again this spring you take
       Earth's ancient vows anew,
And flower as though a thousand brides
       Tossed their bouquets to you.

Spring 1995

This Wildness Too?
Margaret N. Lewis

Across the woods the winds of laughter spill
To start one last, bright-bannered leaf to sway,
Soar free just once, and then sail down until,
In amber swirls, it settles to decay.

Our hands, now burrowed in my pocket, share
A language of their own. Their warmth denies
The fallen leaf, the silver in our hair—
Change natural as a star that burns and dies.

But this! this quiet wilderness, these trees,
Like organ pipes of pagan gods, they rise
To burst high into sunlit melodies
Of twigs that ring against the vibrant skies.
Will all this grace and freedom vanish when
This wildness too must die, cut down by men?

Spring 1995

The Spider's Filigree

Margaret N. Lewis

The bonds of love are frailer than
        The spider's filigree
That glistens in the morning sun
        Like filaments of steel,
Or shows its architectural strength
        Outlined with drops of dew,

For glances cannot shake a web
        Nor brush away one drop,
Yet just one look and one returned
        Can knit a bond for life.

Two lovers' growing interchange,
        Shuttle of look and word,
Can weave a sheltering tent more fair
        Than young Arachne could.

Lovers, beware! Her arrogance
        Shrivelled both weaver and web,
A web whose tatters then could form
        Only a shroud for love.

Spring 1995

Moon
Margaret N. Lewis

The moon has mass so very small
it hasn't any air at all.
Caused by this atmospheric lack
its sky in day and night is black
where stars are always shining bright
by sunlit day or earthlit night.
There were no clouds nor blessed rain
above moon's rocks and dusty plain
when men explored, as mankind must.
Did once a bolt of Martian might
tear from Earth's stony rib and crust
our lovely Lady of the Night?

Fall 1995

Venus
Margaret N. Lewis

In Venus once I used to thrill
and hope that there we might find still,
beneath her clouds that cover much,
a swamp with dinosaurs and such.
But now they say her opaque sky
is dust and poison gas blown high,
her rocks in strength and hardness beat
Earth's stone, or even best concrete,
and Venus' plains are hotter far
than kitchen ovens ever are.

Fall 1995

In Any Language
Thelma Magaril

This happened in an earlier time in a small village, though here and now will do.

Rabbi Aaron Moishe Ashkernazy was known beyond his own village, cherished and respected for his profound decisions, his kindness and philanthropy. His wife, too, was well known, alas, as a shrew and a nag.

This morning, Rabbi Ashkernazy said to his wife, "Lieber Malkah (which means Beloved Queen), I would like my favorite for breakfast, a bowl of barley." Whereupon she served farfel noodles. Yes, with sugar and cinnamon, but not the barley. Another morning, he might ask for farfel noodles and she would serve lentil beans. And so it went on.

Their son, Hillel, dismayed and embarrassed by his mother's contrariness at the breakfast table, one morning reached the kitchen ahead of her, made a huge bowl of barley and placed it before his father, his lips pressed inward and his eyes shining and expectant.

The rabbi, with a faint softening of his face muscles, looked at the bowl of barley, then at his son, and with his raised forefinger waving from side to side as a metronome, quietly said to his son,

"Never interfere in a marriage."

Spring 1990

Poetry
Thelma Magaril

Remember jumping into the piles of autumn leaves, the crackling sound and the smell, the fragrance of burning leaves on the front lawn, and the crisp color of the day?

Well, I don't. I was a city child. I remember the smell of mink, jumping into a huge basket of mink skins, waiting for my mother to have her coat fitted. I inhale deeply. There is silky softness and warmth and my mother within the skins.

I lie there a while, in the aura of contentment that pervaded those moments throughout the shop-loft.

The furriers, too, stop their work for that same while. Everyone is smiling. My mother at my happy play and the gentle workers, the furriers, one can imagine, see their own plump children, and through the corner of their senses, are lifted by a child's enjoyment of their work.

In later times, when I go to my mother's armoire, a handsome two-door mahogany closet where special things are hung, I nuzzle her coat, close my eyes, and know love.

Spring 1990

Old Actor Buddies
(from the Second Avenue Theatre, New York City)
Thelma Magaril

Home from school in my gym suit and books under my arm, I step into my father's store and see him comfortably seated in his nook, speaking with a stranger across the counter.

With lowered eyelids, in passing, I note the stranger as in a one-take camera shot. He is wearing a pearl-gray suit. In his right hand he dangles a hat of pearl gray edged with a white ribbon. His fingernails glow on his pink hands. That his hair is blond adds up to gorgeous.

I go to the family table at the rear of the store. As soon as the stranger leaves, I run to my father, hands out before me, fingers spread and shaking like a puppy pleading. I say, "Papa! Who is that man? Did you see his hands?"

My father, with a mischievous glint in his eye, pausing before each sentence, says, "That was my old actor buddy. I just made four hundred dollars. . . . You see, he asked me for five hundred . . . but I only gave him one!"

Spring 1991

Sunday Mood
Thelma Magaril

Once upon a time a Kissing Breeze loved me. Fresh green leaves on their twisted branches formed my chair where I sat in warm lassitude, tingling with the soft touch on my shoulders, lazily going down my outstretched arms where my clasped hands rested between my knees. I was loved.

And with time, there were astronomy, zoology, optics, medicine, accountancy and chemistry in full color, and such fun, such fun. The world was viewed in youthful ways.

On Sunday, the house was quiet. I was lonely. The window opened wide, I saw the prized, crisp daffodils. Would the blossoms bloom again for me?

Sitting in that same position as long ago, my outstretched arms before me, my hands clasped, across the small wood kitchen table, my thoughts on the wild blue flowers in the field and lilacs at the kitchen door, I felt your presence hovering at my shoulder. Come forward, K.B. I need you—I'll always need you!

Ah . . . your sigh tells me I'm loved.

Fall 1992

Red Spiders at the Loeb
Thelma Magaril

I had the perfect theater seat,
The center of fifth row,
And, so ensconced, it did appear
The play was all for me
And, fused into each actor's part,
The drama's easy flow
Had prompted me to say these words:
"You fool, Don Alvardé,
This pretty girl, euphoria's youth—
You do defy your fate;
This paradox of pleasure . . . stop!"—
It's I must stop this prate.
I came to see a famous play—
For me to act, too late.

Fall 1993

This Time
Thelma Magaril

Why lament
You saw summer skies
And looked upon the seven stages

You say
The children all have flown
Despair Outrageous

Tut tut
Stave away your fears of loneliness
This time is known as Freedom

Fall 1996

Madame Cézanne

Frances McCormick

Ah! Madame!
your charm
suspended
mid shattered, shimmering
surfaces—
arrested, timeless—
so still
you are,
so patient—
thinking of later?
or before?
now
your pensive gaze
remains—
your presence,
wrapped in faceted jacket
and lustrous
striped taffeta,
leans into
yet moves out of
a soft, velvety,
red armchair.

Fall 1995

Bartlett Street Crows

Frances McCormick

This morning
very early
the cacophony
of crows
jars me awake
with its urgency,
its desperation
and its power.
The harsh calls continue
for several minutes
as two large flocks
in trees
a block apart
exchange information.
The caws vary in volume,
intensity
and form.
Dissonant and harsh,
yet clearly full of meaning
to each one of the
jittery, flapping, strutting,
ebony-feathered birds.
Abruptly it ends.
Territory has been claimed,
enemies located, and food.
Marriages arranged,
births announced, and deaths.
Crow's nest treasures bragged about
and the weather discussed.
The sun has been called up.
The day can begin.

Fall 1996

Life
Charles Moore

From years long past
Life flows its placid way
And compassionately looks at us today.
Men have risen to conquer the earth
Men's blood has dyed the waters red,
But Life, unheeding the strife,
Flows calmly on instead.

Spring 1978

Me, Lear
Richard Paine

My children three,
Ever so dear to me,
Are not so dear
As in former times
And other climes.
I'm grown, like Lear, sere.
I am become in name only 'Dad'.
One would be tempted to call the situation sad,
Were it not for this—
(there's consolation in this)—
My daughters still greet me with a kiss,
And my son with less of a hiss!
But I know in my heart of hearts,
They'd really not miss their dad
Were he buried 'neath the caverns of Carlsbad!

Robert Frost knew the feel
Of this particular notch on Fortune's wheel,
And so did Shakespeare's Lear:

"You do me wrong to take me out o' the grave,
Thou art a soul in bliss; but I am bound
Upon a wheel of fire, that mine own tears
Do scald like molten lead."

Spring 1988

Is My Face Red?

Richard Paine

Is it mere poetic fancy,
Or is some tiny bit of me Red Indian?

My kid sister says "No!"
But she remembers not,
Or else has forgot,
Or perhaps heard not,
What I wot:
Whence we were begot.

My grandfather told me
(I think I'm sure he did,
When I was a kid)
That way back in our family
Was a *real American*!

What tribe? Who knows?
Like firewood and kindling,
After the dying glow
Who can ever know
Whence the provenance?

But who can deny me
Just one Iroquois
Or Mohawk
Or Erie?

Spring 1991

The Poets Speak of the Poet's Task

Richard Paine

As Plato in his wisdom said,
"The unexamined life" is dead!

'Tis treason to the human race
To drink Pierian Springs of Thrace

And then attempt not to convey
Arcadian views of yesterday,

Or other insights of delight
To those of us of lesser sight.

And Milton's blindness sonnet too
Elucidates for us that view.

The poet gives and gives again,
Enriching thus his fellow men.

As Robert Browning knew full well,
The poet's task is but to tell

His magic visions, not to hold
Them bottled up till they turn cold.

"A man's reach should exceed his grasp,"
The sage observed o'er demi-tasse.

All this knew Frost and Eliot,
And Blake, and Poe, and Keats, and Scott.

Did Shakespeare's better angels hide
Whole worlds of dreams locked up inside,

Withholding from us, with false o'erweening pride,
That beacon torch, still burning, beaming wide?

Spring 1992

D'Où Venons-Nous? Que Sommes-Nous? Où Allons-Nous?

Richard Paine

This just happened.
I just now learned that the reason
Why my phone call to John White was unanswered.
He had just died.
Obviously, he knew it was coming better than I.
John had a strong affinity with things of the sky,
Living, as he did, hard by
Harvard Observatory.

Then Shakespeare came to mind:
          ". . . something after death . . ."
Now you may not believe this,
But on the first ring of that phone call
I knew something was amiss.

Now I have deciphered John's transmission.
John wanted us all to understand his mission.
It was to ask ourselves, seriously,
Where did he go?

How many times have John and I parlayed over the phone?
So many exchanges of mind!
To what address has he taken my share of this?
To what addresses will we all who knew him take our shares in him?

Fall 1992

My True Love Doth Me Mate
Richard Paine

My true love, when she plays a game,
        Across from me doth sit.
She always beats my pants off . . . shame!
        I'm no match for her wit!

It must be that she casts a spell,
        Especially on my queen,
Because when I think I've done well
        My queen's no longer seen!

My true love has a way with her.
        She offers me her knight.
She makes me think I'm now her bur
        And given her a fright.

And then, you see, from out nowhere
        Her bishop's drawn a bead
Upon my castled king's fast lair . . .
        It never does to plead!

Before I can retaliate
        Her queen's sewed up my fate,
And then she does me osculate,
        And whispers soft, "Checkmate!"

Spring 1993

Waiter Waits Waiter

Richard Paine

I love to go a-dining out
       A-treating all my friends,
Nor stop before, to figure out
       How far my budget bends.

I would not mind it half so much
       If when the check came due,
I hadn't had to wait and wait
       And pay in Time lost too.

So many minutes do I pay
       Our seats to be shown to,
So many more, I have to say,
       The waiter's eyes to view.

The conversation starts to lag
       About the time that he
Returns to tell us that they're out
       Of menu item three.

We send him back to substitute
       A this for a that and then
We settle back . . . another wait . . .
       And wonder if and when

We'll ever see him ere his shift
       Has ended . . . or before
Our appetites we have quite lost . . .
       And all begun to snore!

Spring 1993

In Memoriam—ad Futurum

Milton Paisner

Where'er we look we see a vacant space
That once was filled with a familiar face,
And though we're sad because they're gone from view,
The thought of them refreshes all anew
Because of what they meant to us. They brought
Us comradeship and joy, and so we ought
To temper grief with happiness that they
Did live among us once. The words we say
Today remind us that we too will die
One day. Will those we leave behind just sigh
And say "Goodbye" and then forget that we
Were here? Or will their thoughts about us be
On the same plane as ours about those friends
Departed but still here with us? As life ends
We look back at our years. Not satisfied
With what we view? There's time to look inside
Ourselves to see what we can do before
Whoever has the key shuts tight the door.

Spring 1991

The Door without a Key

Nicholas Prasinos

It is the end of day—the afterbirth.
Another day of mine retreats
Into another twirl of earth—
Into half empty streets.
Visions of what once was within me swell:
The old theatre Durell—
The Elite Café and the ice-cream store
By a stroke of progress are no more.
Where once stood sculptured dreams
Of my devise
Twin arches of McDonald's rise.
There near Banks Street
Where Harvard dormitories stand
I played baseball on once empty land.
These dim remembered days now flown
From earth, to mystic puzzles yet unknown;
They're in my heart indelibly ingrown.
These days that still hold fast
Behind a door without a key,
How they do torture me!
I know that someday they shall all return
With a laughing way from stern
Repositories of my past—
The sadness in my voice,
The faces that I've left—at last
Erase them and rejoice.

Spring 1989

Regrets
(with apologies to François Villon)
Nicholas Prasinos

In this rude life we travel and forget
Like bubbles of a vanished wine;
For alcohol I've drunk, I've no regret—

Songs of the bouzouki and the clarinet
Replaced now by a boogie-woogie whine—
Feasts of lamb bits en brochette

Washed down with swigs of anisette
Now gone—all gone into a sacred shrine.
For those times past, I've no regret.

I've had my fill of life, and yet—
I long for grapes left lingering on the vine.
There were two eyes once emerald set

And lips proffered without regret
That were but for the asking mine.
I hesitated for some tinsel to beget,

Some frothy bauble—I forget
And left the maiden saturnine.
For those days gone, I have regret.

There were two roads upon an apex met:
One lofty with a steep incline;
The other on a level plain was set.

I chose to travel one with little sweat
And follow in a trodden line.
For such decisions, I have deep regret.

Like Ozymandias in a desert set,
I walked almighty in my youth's design.
I could not hear the wind and sand abet

The taunting twirl of time's roulette
That cast my pearls to swine.
For such deaf ears I have a deep regret.

Ah! Trifles these! And yet—
When washed in gallons of erasing wine,
In bourbon, rye or anisette,
They linger on with lone regret.

Spring 1990

A Flower Intricate and Rare
Nicholas Prasinos

I saw a flower intricate and rare
As summer snow with swirls of halo blue
and flecks of random gold inlaid with care
Upon a tapestry of violet hue;

And it grew wild as wind on desert blown
Without a regimen of daily care.
This radiant flower in gentler climates grown
A multi-splendored progeny could bear.

I plucked it from its stark forbidding home
And planted it in science-tested loam.
It died for desert dunes and sunkissed dome.

Fall 1991

The Roller Coaster

Nicholas Prasinos

What would you give, my friend!
What would you give to see
the giant roller coaster
rolling up and down the heights
of old Nantasket Beach
just one more time?

What would you give to hear
crowds screaming in delight
to wild unfettered flight
above the sideshows, the flying horses
and the hurdy-gurdy playing?

What would you give
to feel the anticipation of excitement
only youth can reach,
as you climb aboard again—
echoes of doubt ringing with every footstep
while buttocksing and breasting your way
to claim the one remaining seat?

What would you give
to be a part once more
of that monolithic crowd
still half in dream—
your first love by your side—
swaying in unison
to the hypnotic rock
of tons of wheel and steel?

What would you give, my friend,
for all of this
which sang in us
on this one-way street of time
for one brief moment—
and only one thin dime?

Spring 1994

The Alzheimer's Quartet
Jerome Pressman

I. The Children

Is this our father? This man folded here,
Strapped, perspiring in wheelchair, chin hugging chest.

Facing, unseeing, unspeaking, the TV Celtics game,
Which many nights he cheered, jumping from his chair.

You were strong, fun, full of jokes.
Now spit on face, broken teeth, and urine smell.

We cannot bear to see you as you are.
You are someone else, not he who gave us strength.

Why have you done this to us? We are ashamed.
We must forget you, so that we may survive.

And yet we miss you, and cannot kill our love.
For this would be to kill ourselves. We understand.

II. The Employee

He was a nice guy, very much alive, a good boss, and bright,
Ran a good shop, expanded, kept the overhead down.

I liked him—why didn't I visit him earlier? I'm not that cold.
Perhaps I was afraid for myself. We're all a little crazy.

There he sits—he even used to stand answering his mail.
Kept two secretaries busy; turned out memos by the score.

The doors are locked, no nurses now, the orderlies are gone.
I am not afraid, but tears come trickling down my cheek.

I'll wait my twenty minutes out, keep talking.
If only he would respond.—What do I say? What do I do?

Perhaps I won't come back, might as well forget.
He really doesn't know that I am here. Time to leave.

III. The Wife

Are you inside, listening, comprehending, or just a ghost?
Not even a person, more than less a spouse.

I sleep untouched in the house we built; unspoken now
Our dreams, mere whispers in the wind-bent leaves.

Last time I visited, you said, "What do you know about that?"
After months of no words, just twisted face and broken teeth.

I know you are there, changed, transmuted reverse-wise.
But I must think of myself since you cannot.

I remember your cleverness, subtlety—and the jokes.
The young intern nurse said, "You are a nice man."

We shared the children, house, many sparkling days.
I will not forget you and your love.

IV. The Father

Yes! Yes! I am he who is strapped here. Or
That which has become my 'I'. Which is what?

I remember mostly shadows and lights in waves.
I know you. I think. Curious, you fade.

Who answers my mail? Takes my dog out?
Calculates the overhead at my office?

I feel mostly nothing, but mostly rage
that I have become my own prison-cage.

Touch me, I cannot respond, but touch me.
If I clasp you fiercely do not be afraid.

Forget me, for I am dead. No, do not forget!
Which is it I want? I forget.

Fall 1986

Poetica Mathematica Principia
(after *Mathematica Principia*
by B. Russell and A. Whitehead)
Jerome Pressman

I. The Most Interesting Geometrical Objects

People
Are the most interesting
geometrical objects.
Kinetic sculptures,
Moving windless.
Touch them,
And they respond,
Most times.

Soft sculpture,
Bone armature,
Fleshy tones.
Boldly designed
Holistic structures.
When stressed,
Emitting sounds.

Provenance unknown,
Decaying unloved.
Self-evolving,
Sensual.
People
Are the most interesting
Geometrical objects.

II. Dyadic Variations

I dance the one-two in egoistic variations.
Uno,
I dance it for you, you, you, not me. Don't you see.
Duo,
I dance it for you and me, for you and me, still not free.

Duo Reverso,
I dance it for me and you, for me and you, not quite through.
Penultimo,
I dance it for me, me, me, in harmony, harmony.
Ultimo, ultimo,
I dance it for all of us, all of us. Marvelous, marvelous.

III. The World Is a Prime Number

The world is a prime number,
Indivisible,
Except by it and me,
No factor de-composing.
Grain-galaxy, love-hate, you-me,
Fixed in solidity.

In an opening in the grass the lion strangles his prey.
The flat-chested ballet dancer pirouettes on point.
In her slotted crib a child's hand reaches out.
Men raise tall towers in the sunshine of strange cities.

The world strengthens, throwing out new strands,
Space curves bending back on me.
I am all integral,
I am a prime number.

IV. I Am Invariant under Transformation

I am invariant under transformation.
Pot-belly, gray-hair, unsteady feet, uncertain heart,
Where once flat, black, steady and sure.
Yet this place deep within remains fixed, unaltered.

My child looks out through rheumy eyes.
I am not the same yet more the same.
My hostile mirror on the bureau lies.
In the dust-free mirror of my mind,
I see my true self, pure, unchanged.
I am invariant under transformation.

Spring 1989

The New Exodus

Jerome Pressman

We are all captives in Egypt,
Hebrews and Gentiles alike.
May the lamb's blood be smeared on every doorway
So that the Angel of Death may smite none,
That we may share a common Passover.

We are all wanderers in the wilderness.
May manna descend again to still our hunger
And water flow from rocks to ease our thirst.
Let the pillar of smoke and fire guide us
That we may all find our way.

We are all seekers of the Promised Land.
Our paths may differ—mine East and yours West of Edom and Moab.
We must march through the hostile tribes of Og and Sihon
To reach the sacred soil upon which to rest,
That we may end together in joy and exultation.

May we all be redeemed together,
Or none at all!

Spring 1990

The Best Way

Jerome Pressman

And God Said:

I won't put light in the world.
I'll create shadows
So that people can see the light.

I'll make a dancing world,
But I won't dance.
I'll be the choreographer.

I won't put compassion in the world.
I'll create human beings
And let them invent it.

I will put fear in the world.
It must be first
So that courage may have a place.

I won't put innocence in the world.
I'll make children
And let them be it.

I will put suffering in the world
So that people will know I'm there
When I'm absent.

A little indirection is the best way.

Fall 1991

When Angels Dare No Longer Play

Jerome Pressman

When angels dare no longer play
With freedom clear on needle's head,
Then love itself has lost the day.

For gravity on our thoughts will lay
And unicorns will soon be dead
When angels dare no longer play.

When imagination has no sway
And dreams have thus been put to bed,
Then love itself has lost the day.

The eye behind the eye can't say,
Ah, life; Ah, love, and fear be fled,
When angels dare no longer play.

A narrowed mind says only, Nay—
To darkness, not light, 'tis surely wed;
Then love itself has lost the day.

The world speaks what we make it say:
Speak orange for blue, purple for red.
When angels dare no longer play,
Then love itself has lost the day.

Fall 1993

Homo Sum
Frederick A. Rojak

I am not made of steel,
For steel would snap
Under the steady stress and strain,
Day in, day out, without respite, still another day.

I am not made of steel.
My iron pump, under the unrelenting friction
With the world, would melt,
And, molten, turn me into worthless scrap.

I'm only flesh and blood,
So, under load,
I merely bend
And thus refuse to break.

Spring 1986

Cleaning Up
Bernice Rosenbaum

Friends, if I betrayed you, I didn't mean to
So little time and not much space—
Only in ourselves (if we're lucky)—
Today I read your letters for the last time,
I pressed the flowers of our friendship
Firmly in the folds of my mind
Then, with rapier fingers, I ran your letters through . . .
I thought of those zealots of Masada
Who put their loved ones to the sword
Not to fall into unloving hands.

Fall 1985

Haiku
Bernice Rosenbaum

~   Three lines of black birds
    ~   In flight across a page white
       ~   With unwritten words.

Spring 1986

Highflyers
Kingsley Sanders

I

Icarus, on waxen wings
Soared aloft, the poet sings.
Hardly had his flight begun,
He flew a bit too near the sun,
Melted the wax, and suddenly
Plunged into the Aegean Sea.
For centuries 'twas the reason why
People were too scared to fly.

Of flying men had had their fill.
And that was how it stayed until
In Nineteen Four a Mr. Wright
Endowed us with the power of flight.
Today each son that we have wrought
Wants to be an Astronaut.
I fear now I must end my song.
There hasn't been a Mr. Wrong.

II

Héloïse, declared the bard,
Seduced by Peter Abelard.
He, a Jesuit intellectual,
Adept in matters heterosexual,
Wore no pants beneath his habit,
Sought to emulate the rabbit.
Héloïse was blonde and sultry.
What they did was called Adult'ry.

She, betrayed while having fun,
Was sentenced to become a nun.
Peter, with his reputation
For casuistic disputation,
Proceeded, as a skilled logician,
To argue with the Inquisition.
No matter how well he disputered,
Peter Abelard was neutered.

III

Josephine and Bonaparte
First together, then apart.
Bonaparte and Josephine,
Had a great time in between.
Till he struggled back from Russia,
Pursued by Wellington and Blucher,
Then imprisoned, after trial,
Upon a Mediterranean isle.

Whence he escaped, perhaps released
(The island wasn't strictly policed).
Bony, as soon as he was free,
Galloped back to Gay Paree.
Wellington, with a view-halloo,
Caught him again at Waterloo.
This time, without even tellin' 'er,
They sent Napoleon to St. Helena.

Fall 1996

Remembrance
Rita A. Sheehan

Lilacs,
poignant scented
blooms, recall springtime joys
we shared before I learned to walk
alone.

Spring 1982

Iter Cantabrigia
Rita Skinner

She's a senior and spry on her feet,
But the pavement's a lopsided street.
So, with cane in her hand
She'll make sure she'll withstand
The heaves and the holes that she'll meet.

There are cracks in the sidewalk to tread;
There are craters she sees up ahead.
So, with eyes on the ground
And not one look around,
She'll make sure all her fears have been shed.

Oops!

Spring 1992

in the silent place
Rhea Sossen

I found a river
without ripples

chose a flower
for its whispering

planted a rock
below a cloud

and listened

Fall 1994

Morning Lights the Backdrop

Rhea Sossen

Whiffs of red cedar lead
to a rainforest dense
with giant fern crowded
by the plane-train roaring
of an avalanching
river and chilled air leads
to icefield majesties
slowly grinding dripping
into blue-green glacial
lakes and flashes of pink
lead to fireweed fields
amid surviving spruce
and Douglas fir give way
to skyscraper falls where
mountain goats may drink
where black-billed magpies sing
in sunlight and dark light.

Spring 1996

Whose Villanelle Is This, Anyway

Rhea Sossen

Too many details fill each day.
From midnight to midnight you dot all the i's.
Stop it, halt and turn away

from unmatched buttons, a collar that's frayed,
smudges in the dustpan, garbage that you prize.
So many details spoil your day:

grass in the dandelions, a nasty cat that strays
(let her get lost, she's a tigress in disguise).
Stop. Now. Time drifts away

while you read all the junk, debate what to pay,
check all sources to figure out who lies.
Too many details squander your days.

Work in the underground or skydive for play.
Gamble with strangers at games you devise.
Then stop, laugh and turn away.

Throw out crumbled cookies, papers that say
nothing, except who lives or dies.
All these details empty the day.
Stop the drainage. Move away.

Fall 1996

Pessimists
Harold Stubbs

Some folks maintain that life's a cruel joke,
That all our earnest labor counts for naught.
These gloomy ones are likely to invoke
Old Thomas Gray, whose Elegy once taught
That "paths of glory lead but to the grave."
And others say the world goes fast downhill,
And though man *has* made progress from the cave,
The atom bomb may put him back there still.
Or if by chance we may escape from that
(These doomsday prophets claim), all signs portend
Pollution will destroy our habitat
And scarce resources soon will reach an end.
I get so mad I almost want to fight
These pessimists—but then I fear they're right.

Spring 1996

Snowstorm
Rowland Sturges

The rafters shook with such a blow
White fury swirling high and deep
Enormity of wind and snow

A sunrise cast a feeble glow
We slowly rose up from our sleep
The rafters shook with such a blow

As we watched it slowly grow
And make a sudden vaulting leap
Enormity of wind and snow

With all that's past, Lord help us grow,
In future winter's fastness keep.
The rafters shook with such a blow
Enormity of wind and snow.

Spring 1992

Ars Rhetorica Vincit Omnia

Alex Sutton

(Success guaranteed in any sector—private, public, or extra-terrestrial)

If you're faced with a problem, that will not go away
To which you have no answer, then here's the way to play.

You just rely on Rhetoric.
It's a winner every time.
Put your trust in Rhetoric:
It won't cost you a dime.

Seek out and find a nifty phrase, which doesn't grate the ear.
Speak it with conviction—Say it loud and clear.

You cannot lose with Rhetoric.
It's a winner every time.
Have faith—have faith in Rhetoric.
It doesn't cost a dime.

Shout it from the housetops—murmur it at tea;
Never change the wording—never change the key.

We all depend on Rhetoric.
It saves us every time.
What's cheaper than plain Rhetoric?
It doesn't cost a dime.

If you're running for an office and you haven't got a clue
As to the major issues—then here is what you do:

Just fill the air with Rhetoric.
It's the best thing every time.
Don't turn your back on Rhetoric;
It won't cost you a dime.

Fall 1989

Timor Mortis Conturbat Me
Alex Sutton

Timor mortis conturbat me.
I read this phrase recently
and it disturbed me,
not because I fear death
but because I fear accountability.
It was made very clear that I did not possess
the avenue of escape of deniability.
Looking back, I saw so many things
that had outraged me.

I also saw that too often
I had done nothing.
In other cases I had made a protest
but nothing beyond that.

As I thought more and more
it became blindingly clear
that the phrase that bothered me
should have read:
Amor Christi conturbat me.

Fall 1991

My Zoo Is the Best Zoo
David Todd

There is a zoo not far from me
That aunts and uncles like to see.
They take me there and give me dimes
For parrot food—and ofttimes
We see the lion in her cage;
But she is never in a rage.
In fact, she sleeps the whole day through—
The same for tigers, hippos too.
My aunts and uncles have such fun
Watching deer that never run.
It's a pity they don't see
The beasts that really live for me!
In my back yard I watch the ants
That never stop their lively dance:
It's in and out and up they go,
Never stopping, never slow.
When tired of them I look up high
and see the creatures in the sky.
That cloud's a whale—this a bird;
They change each moment; it's absurd
To say they're not alive at all!
They twist and turn, they rise and fall;
In half a wink a cow is gone
And in her place a sheep is born.
What was a snake gets awfully fat
And soon becomes a Cheshire Cat.
The zoo? Oh poo! I have my own.
My creatures need no bars or walls,
No keepers wash their pens and stalls—
And I enjoy them all alone!

Spring 1993

My Father's House
Frances Downing Vaughan

Something is skewed. I am older
than my father ever was.
All these years
the windows and porches of the house
watching the Rappahannock River
where he played on Sharp's sagging wharf,

and once I played under the wharf
housekeeping with my older
cousins, poured water from the river
full tin to empty tin, it was
standing here, the family house
where he spent his straitlaced boyhood years.

Though it's been more than sixty years
and only pilings hint a wharf,
I recognize the house
still staring, only older,
sagging a bit, paint flaking, as
he must have seen it, steaming down-river

en route to the Hudson River
and West Point—those uniform years
as cadet, instructor; it was
waiting. His parents at Sharp's wharf
would greet him (now medalled, older),
the familiar upright house

welcoming. Then we at the house,
my father explaining lights on the river;
my brother (his namesake), older
than me by some six years,
tying his skiff to the wharf.
This was

all I had of my father—he was
dead before I was eight. The house
may hold footprints, the wharf
collapsed; the persistent river
rising, lowering all these years
effacing us, tides older.

I take a pebble that was washed up by the river
in front of the house. I hold it, turning those years
under the wharf so my father is older.

Spring 1990

Yellow-Crowned Night Heron
Frances Downing Vaughan

Where the unruffled water,
feather gray,
reflects his plumage,
he stares back,
searching among mirrored reeds
for his stalklike legs
detectable only
when someone nears the pond
as I do now,
trembling grasses,
but, startled,
he steps forward
and loses track.

Spring 1990

The Pink House

Frances Downing Vaughan

Each summer's seen the pink house fade
and tilt a little more
until it's taken on the shape
of the old lobsterman we used to meet
making his way to the store, ninety if he was a day,
legs bowed from holding himself upright
hauling traps on heaving boats,
only no islander would paint
the clapboards of his house pale pink,
window-trim magenta as the rugosa roses
blooming and tumbling
from the weight of their lush growing.

This was an artist's house.
One day a sign goes up:
Closed for All Seasons.

Shoulder strapped,
enveloped by serape,
he's had a fall.
"But that's not all," he says,
invites me in,
studio hung with Persian yarn—
orange, fuchsia, shades of pink and purple lupine,
blues of sea.

"Do you know the gypsies' paterand?" he asks,
"Well, you know a cairn?
Gypsies place these things for signs:
'That farmer's got a horse' or
'Over there there's corn'.
I should have known,
I got these signs:
two friends I saw in Mexico,
my eyes gone bad—
I'd not have come at all this year,
I must return me to my source."

He doesn't want the casserole,
so much food they throw it out.
I, who would prop up his house,
repaint it shining pink,
set a fat new tomato atop each green bottle
on the kitchen windowsill
and give him eyes again for weaving,
all I can do is mark
how paint flakes curl as petals from a rose.

Spring 1990

Happy the Well-To-Do Barnacles
Frances Downing Vaughan

Happy the well-to-do barnacles
here in their winterized tents,
enough space between them
so twice a day, laid back,
fluttering fans,
they wave food in;
close enough
so when the urge comes on
a neighbor's within reach,
and the eggs,
hatching inside everyone,
become little larvae
growing up to wander off,
testing similar sites,
the right light in the tidal zone.

But seething down the rock
where the squeeze is on,
it's hard to hang on—
all the barnacles so skinny
they grow up crooked,
fighting among themselves
when the water comes over
for food.

Sometimes, no one watching,
I lay my head down at the shore,
listening for sense in what's swaying.

Fall 1990

Baghdad
Frances Downing Vaughan

Grief-shawled head bowed over,
you wail your broken heart
beside the rubble
where men crawl one by one
out of the earth
this terrible dawn
bearing blanketed wrecks of bodies.

Under a dark green cover
your sharp eyes spy Jabriel
who used to bear for you
jugs of water from the well,
corral the vagrant goat—
his slender arms still reaching,
but charred to the bone
in this macabre feast for gods of war.

Spring 1991

Encounter in Harvard Square

Frances Downing Vaughan

You put those gloves down somewhere—
the counter at Warburton's,
the steps across the way—
and forgot them? That's O.K.
When I saw you breath-
ing on your fingers
and bought the gloves,
they said you'd only lose them.
You'll get a new pair from me,
or from some other soft touch
in Harvard Square.
Some days, sober,
you recognize me: your eyes light up.
Take care, I say, and mean it,
not being the woman
who would have gone on trusting,
except for the racing form
and your horse coming up loser
again and again,
or the daughter who waits
for father to remember her birthday
again and again.

Fall 1991

Scapegoat
Frances Downing Vaughan

Don't blame me, said the stone
catapulted across the beach,
crashing the window,
scattering glass,
coming to rest against a sodden sofa.
I held the water back a thousand times,
then lost my grip.
I'm left for you to kick;
the water hides.

Fall 1991

Blue Hill
Frances Downing Vaughan

The strength gone out of him,
but not the dignity,
the granite-gray old fisherman
lies beached in a hospital bed
a long cast from Blue Hill Bay,
the call from his daughter a continent away
spinning a line back to Bear Island:

his father's way stood him good stead,
working the outer ledges setting fifty
maybe sixty traps a day,
her makin' the chowda,
the kids coming one after another
then the boy gone—

no sense, racin' cars, rockin' like
the steel dolly rattling
down the corridor to his door.

82

The nurse tucks a bib on him,
sits on the bed to spoon the macaroni salad.
"I'll go home and make you a chowda—no,
I'll bring you scallops, some in the shell . . .
Darlin'," she says, close by his ear,
stretching seams of her purple slacks,
long pigtail swinging,
"Real butta," she whispers and he smiles,
first time today.

Fall 1992

Heirloom
Frances Downing Vaughan

Four maple posts thrust upwards
from the corners of this bed,
penciling stories
where my mother laid her head
on linen pillowcase
embroidered for her trousseau,
where she read mysteries until daybreak—
wan rays creeping across the sill,
moving a band of light across wide floorboards,
dressing table: the oval frame
my father peered from, then
my brother's face, returning
his precious, crooked smile
(both of them long dead);
pale light burnishing shoehorn,
brush matted with silvered hair,
the mirror in which she read
time reflected on her face,
that epic of memories I inherited.

Fall 1993

Pillow-Talk
Frances Downing Vaughan

In the skeleton of Sarajevo
a dark-eyed woman halts,
dragging the small boy with her
into the bones of a doorway.

They killed my husband.
I have my arms and legs, she says;
my heart is dead.
My pillow knows the truth.

Spring 1994

Winter Daybreak, Nantucket
Frances Downing Vaughan

Before the pink returns to sidewalk and chimney brick,
panes still dark where wives of sailors watched,
while except for steamship crew
and taxi cruising cobblestone lanes
the whole town sleeps,
she rises to shake the grate—
children stumble into the kitchen
laughing, tumbling over each other
like live pink coals.

Fall 1996

The Snow Globe

Frances Downing Vaughan

When I got up to pull the window shade
I found white lace had edged the fire escape
Lightly. On the chimney pots the snow had made
Little peaked caps, had traced the elm tree's shape
In gentle strokes along its outstretched arm.
And I remembered, once I had a globe
My hand could hold: in its transparent charm
Viewed snowflakes I could shake to make a robe
Around a man and woman by a tree
Under a bright blue mountain and then,
Gathering flakes upside down, let them fall free
Happily enchanted again, again.
And here I've waked inside this magic dome
Now your love circles me and snowflakes come.

Fall 1996

Lunch at the Harvard Faculty Club

Frances Downing Vaughan

professors undisguised
abstractedly stride by
maitre d'
student waiter from Nigeria
each in his role
under the static gaze
of wealthy and/or distinguished grads
gathered gilt elbow to gilt elbow
someone's once-new Victorian vase
upon the period sideboard
another's candelabra
beside a plate of pickled beets
wisps of conversation
mingle above steam table
drift Karl Barth
Darwinian theory
over this high-graded kingdom
of metaphysics sex
wine cheeses
scholarship
while down the block
in Henry James' old yard
a squirrel digs a tulip bulb
and gnaws away

Spring 1997

Cause of death: coronary occlusion. . . .
Interval between onset and death: seconds
Charles Vivian

Those last few seconds of your consciousness—
What were they like? When in your heart the blood
Was blocked and dammed, then did a sudden guess
Come, and turn swiftly into certitude
That this was death—as if a slab of stone
Sealed off the way out of a cave? What more
Than just this knowledge, this one fact alone
Could there be in your mind a moment for,
While the inexorable darkness came?
Did you, who died on land, in some way know
In one flash all your life's course, just the same
As they say drowning swimmers do? If so,
In all that rush of memory, oh then
I hope my love was there for you again.

Spring 1990

A Sonnet
Charles Vivian

Someone who didn't know her very well
Might see her surface charm, and see no more:
Struck vividly by that, he could not tell—
Not until later, anyway—what store
Of strength and spirit fills her. She has known
The fear of want, for both herself and those
Whom she loved, and who looked to her alone
For nurture and support—and so she rose
Up, and prepared herself, and met their need.
She has heard words of insult and abuse,
Betrayal—until finally she freed
Herself, and set her soaring spirit loose.
The darkness is dispelled; we can see how
The light shines on her and shines from her now.

Fall 1990

Animus in Animalcules?
(Motivation in Pathogens?)
Charles Vivian

Not even to a germ would we ascribe
Deliberate malice, active ill intent;
He gets inside us, and may eat, imbibe
Our fluids—but then, none of this is meant
To hurt us; that is just a side effect.
Then how about a virus—a mere juice,
Which we cannot in conscience even connect
With the idea of a living thing, or use
Any concept of consciousness at all?
If the afflictions bred of viruses
Just seem to make no sense, or if they fall
Into no plan, the reason may be this:
They start out the right way, but then get lost;
They always seem to get their virus crossed.

Spring 1991

Tempora/Mores
Charles Vivian

Even the eighteenth century we call
The Enlightenment, as if the people then
Finally knew the truth—or they knew all
They needed to live life as women and men
Of true humanity: to live in peace.
Now, to be sure, it did not quite work out
That way: neither did all war swiftly cease
Nor other kinds of unpleasantness. No doubt
One would have been naive to anticipate
Otherwise. —But that was two hundred years
Ago. Now we have learned to conquer hate,
Haven't we, and to quell our mutual fears?
We can thank God when we consider how
That kind of thing is all behind us now.

Spring 1991

True Identity?

Charles Vivian

What is it I remember? Did I see
My father coming home from work that day
When I was four years old, bringing for me
A toy? or did I just hear someone say
It happened? I cannot get back inside
That little boy, or look out through his eyes,
Although they once were mine. When I have tried
To feel again, to sense, to recognize
The mind, the self, the consciousness I knew
Even only a year or two ago,
The experience has been like looking through
The wrong end of a telescope. I know
How much the years have brought of difference;
Who shall I be a year or five years hence?

Spring 1992

Past and Present

Charles Vivian

There is the bench where you were sitting— you
And our good friend. And now you are both dead.
How can it be, what is so plainly true,
A stark and open fact, so simply said,
Can still be utterly incredible?
Whenever I pass by that bench again,
Memories strongly come alive, and fill
My mind's eye: I see now what I saw then.
Sometimes the past presses upon us so,
With such intensity and vividness,
That we feel almost that we do not know,
Not where we are, but when we are. We guess,
And scramble with confusion back to now—
Without our really understanding how.

Fall 1992

Old Mortality
Charles Vivian

No young man thinks that he will ever die,
Nor woman either, William Hazlitt wrote.
Labor and love, faith and conviction vie
Each with the other: what shall he devote
His energy and his attention to?
In all the bright kaleidoscope of youth,
Which pattern, which design, which vivid hue
Has most of beauty? of bright or bitter truth?
Never could death (whatever that is) touch
His going on forever with the dance
Of ceaseless, swift activity. So much
For young men in their happy ignorance.
No old man lives, in firmest fact I find,
Without the knowledge always in his mind.

Fall 1992

The Lore and the Profits
Charles Vivian

How many are there in the world who see
One maxim they consider always true:
Anyone who is different from me
Is wrong, and probably subversive too.

Spring 1993

Progress
Charles Vivian

If John Keats could come back to life today—
He who walked up and down the corridors
Of Guy's and Thomas' hospitals, where lay
The wounded in their blood, with no recourse
To pain-assuaging medicine, or chance
Of decent, cleanly dressing; he who heard
The cries and groans of those whom circumstance
Had struck with foul disease, or with absurd
Disfigurement; he, too, who smelled the stink
Of excrement and vomit—
                              of a real
Modern-day hospital, what would he think?
But how much difference is there? The ideal
Is to relieve all suffering, and we try,
But people still get sick, and people die.

Fall 1993

Nature Requites Our Love
Charles Vivian

The earth caresses the soles of my feet;
        The air, like fine white wine,
Is cool and vivid in my mouth;
        The silver sun will shine
Its light and warmth upon my head;
        The wind that sails along
Sounds in my ears and in my heart
        Its lovely wayward song.

Spring 1994

Untitled
Charles Vivian

If I have lived these many years with you
(These many by the calendar, though few
And short, and golden by the heart), if this
Has made no minor metamorphosis
At least, in me; if I look out upon
Our world, but not as you do; if I con
The faces of our friends and others there
Without more empathy, or warmer care:
If this is how I am, what have I earned
But shame for lovely lessons never learned?

Spring 1997

Irish Fancies: Noises in the Night
Dorothy Sprague Wadman

Why is it, I wonder,
As soon as I get in bed and settle
Myself for a good sleep
The house starts creaking and snapping and groaning at me;
And footsteps pad softly down the corridor and stop
At my door—just outside—
But no hand grasps the door knob, Thank God,
For my heart a-thumping as it is against my ribs
Might give up altogether.

Is it ghosts? Or leprechauns? Or what is it?
And who lives in the cellar
Sleeping all day and waking in the night
To grab a hammer and whack away
At the pipes?

And I'd like to know—
Is there a spirit in wood that wants out?
Are there gnomes in metal calling it back underground?
Do nails cling to rafters with a will by day
But loosen their hold in darkness?
Does the spirit of *house* dance in the attic?

And is it the voice of one who died here
In this place, in this house that whispers
       "Sleep . . . sleep;
       What do you have anyway
       Better than sleep?"

Spring 1988

"They Broke a Merry Thought Together"*
Farley W. Wheelwright

"They broke a merry thought together,
       Mr. Copperthwaite and Kate,
And Kate got the largest part,
       Upon which the color rose and spread
Over the gentleman's wide beautiful forehead."

What merry thought, do you suppose, that Katie said
       Caused poor old Copperthwaite to turn beet red?
Did she have ideas, perhaps did she suggest
       Something proper ladies never said—even in jest?

Mayhap he thought the merry conversation
       Was hinting at some future location
And filled him with much agitation
       To contemplate a very un-Victorian assignation—

* A line from a story written in the form of a diary and discovered in Peterson's *Ladies' National Magazine*, dated June 1861.

The diary does not say.
       But the last entry for that day
Writ by another who at the table sat,
       Gives evidence that the diarist was
A bit of a jealous cat.

"Kate was very lovely," she wrote,
       "In her gown
Of fine mauve merino and black trimmings.
       But I have seen her appear to
Better advantage." End quote.

Thus the merry thought they broke together,
       Mr. Copperthwaite and Kate,
Seemed less than merry to another.
Could it have been a touch of unmerry satire
       Writ in spite by another of Copperthwaite's lovers?

If so those merry thoughts were a kind of fun
I did not think was invented
In eighteen hundred sixty-one.

Fall 1996

Damn!
John White

I can manage my bifocals
To my dentures I'm resigned
I can live with my arthritis
But I do so miss my mind!

Fall 1986

In Unity
(I did but touch it passing by . . .)
John White

A little stickiness is a dreadful thing
in fact there is no such thing
as a little stickiness—
like pregnancy, death,
or a from-an-airplane fall
it is all or nothing at all
a state which you are or you are not in
and right this minute
courtesy of this raspberry jam
ugh
in it
I am
damn
I wipe these fingers on this handkerchief these socks this
shirt
these pants
everything
I even run through my hair
but ugh it is still there
that shadow of a breath of a hint of tar-and-featherness
that lousy lousy lousy togetherness
damn stickiness
now I lick them again
swab them strongly with my tongue
bite them scrape them between my teeth
put them under my shoe and grind them in honest dirt
rub and scrub them until they are red hot
and then
tentatively touch them together again
and are they?—they are not—
damnation
still that tiniest suspicion
ugh
of co-ugh-hesion
no
cloth hair tongue teeth grit
will not
do it
nothing will do it

stickiness
dreadful stuff
I should know
you always have to go
and roll up your sleeves—better take off your shirt—
and wash with warm water and soap and rag and
everything
clear to the elbow
and even then
oh well
oh stickiness stickiness
why is it so
why are you such
that such a little of you is so much
how can you, so minusculely microareable,
be so bloody goddamn unbearable?
stickiness
you are so bodacious undealable-with uninfluenceable
unignorable tenacious a resident
you should be president.

Fall 1987

Oxford Dream
Mary Winchester

I dreamt I lay upon my bed;
A sober doctor shook his head;
"The patient's ills are too far gone,
I doubt that she can carry on.
She's filled with Archaeology,
History and Geology;
These, mixed with Sociology,
Strain her Physiology,
Inducing a Pathology,
And, given her Psychology,
I shouldn't be surprised if she
Expires of Philology."

Spring 1979

It's Lovely to Live on a Raft
Mary Winchester

Oh, it's lovely to live on a raft!
Though it's hardly an elegant craft,
Yet, it rides down the river with just the right speed,
And takes you wherever your fancy might lead,
And, drifting along, your spirit is freed;
Oh, it's lovely to live on a raft!

Oh, it's lovely to live on a raft!
Yes, it's cramped, to be sure, fore and aft;
But, at night, all the space between heaven and earth
Is blazoned with stars at Infinity's hearth,
And a man there can measure his life and his worth;
Oh, it's lovely to live on a raft!

Spring 1980

Territorial Imperative
Mary Winchester

The bluejay screams his strident call,
"Get out! Get out, intruders all!
This grove is mine!" So lark and grouse
Avoid the space around his house.

The great baboon guards jealously
His ladies, home, and family;
The daddy seal defends his rock,
And woe to males who try to dock.

The wooden fence with sharp barbed wire,
The thick stone wall with tangled briar,
The modest picket fence you see
—Territoriality?

Spring 1981

Lines to Ronnie from Nancy Lysistrata
(who has become a dove)
Mary Winchester

You returned empty-handed from Iceland,
A fact that I, frankly, deplore;
I had hoped you'd return with a treaty
That would ban war for evermore.

When you left all my hopes rose up soaring,
I thought Mike and you would agree
To cut missiles, now sixty thousand,
To maybe a dozen or three.

But, it seems your intransigent posture
Regarding your dream, S.D.I.,
Is set in your head now in concrete;
You're determined that Star Wars will fly.

And Mikhail is equally certain
That Star Wars means U.S. first strike,
And if you persist he has threatened
His arsenal numbers to hike.

As Lysistrata once called together
The wives and the sweethearts of Greece,
And forced all their husbands and lovers
To stop fighting and cultivate peace,

So, Raisa and I had a meeting
Of women from both of our lands,
And we have agreed to be loveless
Until you grant all our demands.

The cabinet wives also joined us;
They, too, have agreed to resist,
And swear the Potomac will dry up
Before they consent to be kissed.

We also have planned to take over
The Treasury, likewise the taxes;
Your friends at G.E. and at Boeing
Will not have unlimited access.

You'll find me reserved and laconic;
Pursue me, but then I will run;
Our meetings will just be platonic,
And I'll be as chaste as a nun.

My tootsies won't warm your cold ankles,
My lips will remain tight and cold;
You may neither hug nor embrace me;
I'm not yours to have and to hold.

Once, candy was thought to be dandy,
Though licker was quicker, men claimed;
Now the stakes in the game are much higher,
And Peace is the price we have named.

The boycott already is spreading,
To ladies on land and sea;
It soon will affect Reaganomics
And shrivel the whole G.N.P.

Results will affect demographics
The birthrate will register void,
Soon midwives and all obstetricians
Will complain that they're underemployed.

So, you and the world's macho leaders
Had better make sure war will cease,
And when you confer in Geneva
Be certain you make plans for Peace!

Fall 1986

History of Boston

Mary Winchester

Benjamin Franklin, the clever old Yankee,
Was known far and wide for discreet hanky-panky.

Did Paul Revere of daring deed
Call "Hi! Ho! Freedom" to his steed?

Hutchinson, the Boston Tory,
Gained the pelf, but lost the glory.

Samuel Adams, the old Boston smarty,
Stirred up rebellion and gave a tea party.

Little did John Hancock dream
His name to lad and lass
Would come to mean a signature
And flying panes of glass!

At first, Ben Franklin's politics
Seemed a little fright'ning,
But, like *Poor Richard's Almanac*,
They soon caught on like lightning.

Fall 1986

Eliza
Liberty Winter

She plucked
one
white petal
from
the daisy

patiently
tried
putting it
back

unbelieving first
then furious

Fall 1986

Ode to a Tree
Liberty Winter

Nothing so soft, nothing so unattached
as that falling yellow leaf through air,
silently, innocent it must be said,
of its fall. The less and the less
and the less, each morning's sun shines
through a fresh arrangement of leaves—
how pale, how thin and delicate the tree grows.
All that remains is the bittersweet climbing,
the gray stalk winding, twisting around the trunk.
In the yellow metallic berries, now cracked open
and red, a squirrel scolds.

Fall 1986

Ethiopia, 1985
Liberty Winter

I raised my shoulders, shocked to read
that people were ever that cruel.
I was referring to Nero, Caligula,
and others, who needed to be entertained
while eating dinner—by gladiators
taking sideswipes at each other.

While I eat mine to thousand times
thousand their entertainment—
am addicted to it—files and rows and pyramids
of bare, cadaverous, distended bellies,
and no hope in sight for it.
The zebra has fallen over on his side,
and even the camel has had it.
The camera gives his long, twisted mouth in a close-up.

Fall 1987

Out Walking
Liberty Winter

That old man who used to come around
the corner on his bicycle,
leaning forward, I remember,
the air glistening on his skin,
is dead now, and I am thinking of him,
not really, of death, of this street
I'm walking on now, but then, won't be.

Fall 1988

The Somnambulist
Liberty Winter

Ah, but to leave this world and leave no name:
To end like Ozymandias, two solid legs of dirt,
and yet, he lives. The irony's his fame.

I would live on in some fictitious shame.
Say Tess of D'Urbervilles, deserted, badly hurt,
Rather than leave this world and leave no name.

Or I could be remembered as the self-same
Bird Ruth heard, when Naomi she would not desert,
For he sings still in his rhapsodic fame.

There's Cleopatra who can boast being the bane
Of Rome, extravagant as a flirt.
So as she left this world she left her name.

Some say when you are dead it's all the same.
What does it matter, covered over by dirt?
And yet you live when someone says your name.

Let those who think this playfulness is vain
(But there is noble precedent I assert)
For oh, it's sad to leave this world and leave no name,
And so, I'm chasing rainbows after fame.

Spring 1989

Samsara: a Prose Poem
Liberty Winter

She continues looking for the treasure she'd been told her mother had hidden from her. The first spring for a moment she thought she caught a corner of it under a marigold in the garden, but it was always eluding her. And being no fool, she kept telling herself it was only fantasy: nothing had been hidden. But because something more would so much add to what she already had, which was sparse, she thought, considering: the chairs and beds, the lamps, the bird's-eye maple tables, mirrors and linens and what-not-shelves galore. She claimed her sisters had taken everything, she continued looking.

Ten years later, instead of diminishing, this desire for more kept growing in her—her mother filling her out as she did, or in—all wrapped up in the memory of her. Surely she was saying something important to her. One August day when she was wrapping a present to send off to a great-niece who had just graduated from college in Wyoming, she came upon a hard bit of rolled-up tissue in all the masses of papers and boxes she had stored in her attic. She unwrapped it to find the top of a silver flacon. From that day on she got more and more into the search. A good part of every day was spent upstairs in the attic, winter and summer through all kinds of weather, through all the boxes and rolled-up papers. . . .

Spring 1989

Haikus on November

Liberty Winter

Some fall night I must
walk off the edge of the earth
right into the moon

you can't reach the dead
you will stop remembering them
when you are with them

on an autumn beach
I come upon one brown duck
his glass eye is green

the air inside me
the air I feel around me
the same, the same air

to walk along the shore
while hearing only the sound
under my boots change

each time I see
your phone number in my book
I know the page is dead

one gull screams harshly
two gulls scream in unison
three gulls are silent

Fall 1989

A Sestina on a Ring
Liberty Winter

For the entire lunch my mind was on the ring—
a diamond—such a give-away, a bandage
not covering, but exposing, allowing
the third finger of my left hand to sense
where my parents were coming from. Tear-
ful, embarrassed for them. Even for the flowers

on the table. All so festive, but no flowers
to celebrate my new life because of the ring.
I'd just returned home, too stunned for tears,
to hear my parents continue talking with their guests, badinage,
conversations for any day, making no sense
to me, who thought they'd of course, stop, allowing

me my turn. "She's wearing a ring." Allowing
me to stretch my hand out, knock over the flowers,
for now the conversation was making sense:
their daughter home from a visit wearing his ring.
It wasn't because it was he, they bandaged
their eyes from the ring, it was she, she near to tears

known all her life. It still brought her near tears
that her parents thought her unable to love, allowing
exception for dogs and rabbits and cats, all bandage
for the proper love of a daughter. Her mother righted the flowers,
and I hid my hand under the table, hid the ring
for I knew my being engaged didn't make much sense

to them. And the guests staying silent didn't make sense
to me. They couldn't know the long years of close-to-tears
tension at the table. They must have wanted to mention the ring,
but they didn't, perhaps embarrassed, allowing
that with time they sensed that in spite of flowers
this was an inglorious meal, that talk mere badinage.

I held my finger twisted in the napkin like a bandage
for in spite of everything the silence made no sense.
To make such a point of picking up the flowers,
not a word of the ring—my new life. Tears
must have risen to my eyes, allowing
for some love, hopefully found in the ring.

It's a sad little tale of rings and bandages
and flowers. Nothing makes sense to her,
and the censor sitting, disallowing tears.

Fall 1989

Florence
Liberty Winter

Trying on the vow of chastity
he asked her, "How do I look?
Now really . . . I want to know."
Her eyes rested awhile on his navel:
it was dark, but shone like a light
on rocks under water, and around it
lay flesh with a delicate line of fine hair.
The cord of his pants fell down one leg
and his feet were white and strong.
"Do I look . . . would you say . . . classical?"
He frowned slightly, "This fat here."
He took a scolding pinch, held his hand
on his waist, the knuckles curved;
his turquoise had never been so blue.
"You're laughing at me . . . do you like . . . ?"
He laughed then, his throat rippled.
"You've *David*'s head," she had often told him,
and then he would cup her face, and she his hands.
Behind his shoulders through the casement window,
his back against the hills and sky,
"You're beautiful, yes," she told him.

Spring 1990

Daddy

Liberty Winter

He struggled so hard as a person.
Lucky occasionally, he joked black humor,
sitting out his hours in the movie theaters
instead of selling bonds to customers,
praying Jack Kennedy would die the day before
he did, because the country was spending
uneconomically. He had the prayer to show us
in his little black book.

And so goddamn interested in sex
he didn't want to see his favorite blonde granddaughter
when she was illegitimately pregnant. . . .
I felt sorry for the bastard,
his wife and we four daughters treating him
as if he'd never been a lieutenant commander
in two world wars and could wear the uniform still,
his hair trim, red his favorite color.

With all his crazy notions
you couldn't call him devious, like one day
at the age of seventy-nine, because he had
no pension, only life insurance made out
to his second family, instead of going to work,
he stepped in front of the commuting train
with a card of identification on one wrist,
the one that went flying over the grit-filled bank.

Fall 1990

Kindergarten Story Hour
Liberty Winter

> *White as an angel is the English child*
> *But I am black, as if bereaved of light.*
> —William Blake

I keep on wishing Beauty's Beast
will turn out black. I love her so!
Her golden hair, blue eyes and snow-white skin.

And she is brave as well as kind.
I would be really scared
dressed in his heavy cloak, that ugly mask!
>   Don't look at me he says
>   each time he creeps into her bed.
I always peek when sleeping with my mother.

Fall 1990

Memento Mori
Liberty Winter

I. The Three Sisters

When Mother died we tore her house apart.
Of course it was she we pulled and tore,
and yet we could not stop. Joan started us out
each day with silent meditation. And then
like three sleek lions we uncurled our claws.
"I'm sure Mother would like me to have this . . .
to have this . . . and this. . . ." French bracket feet
flanking a valance apron, Samson-footed bowl
with burgundy border, Parian figure barefoot boy.
All appraised there in the inventory.
O, the pity of it. It was as if Mother
watched and wept and does so still.

II. Mother's Plea from the Medical School

"Let my bones rest and reassembled
bury me. For laid out on these shelves
I am estranged from earth.
It was good to continue a little longer
being part of things, good to intrigue.
To see the perplexed brow bent over a tiny piece
of my tissue, to hear my blood beat
in the test tube.
I do not regret my decision, but
let me be done with it now."

Spring 1991

110

A Domestic Affair

Liberty Winter

To Tithonus, son of Laomedon, King of Troy, and brother to
the future King Priam, whose beauty even in those days surpassed
all others. The Goddess Dawn fell in love with him
and, in the rapture of what she told him was her first
real love affair, she begged Zeus to make the young man,
like her, immortal. I wonder, was she so seduced by his looks
that she actually forgot at the same time to ask Zeus
to keep him from growing older?
Was she so seduced by his touch?

From the very beginning the aging process disgusted her.
His long beard, through which she loved to twist
all ten rosy fingers, gone first,
graying a little, then turning white, stiff.
His body shriveling like brown leaves.
His arms too frail to hold her.
But the worst was the change in his voice!
With each new day sounding more like the chirp
of a tiny cicada, that once resonant voice
of his, commanding, rather.

So your saffron-mantled mistress
pushed you further, then further from her.
Out of the bed first, then refusing to sit down with you at table.
Finally packing you off to a distant wing of her house,
to one tiny room, to grow older and older.
Had she not truly thought of this when talking to Zeus,
or could she have wanted to keep the door slightly ajar?

O, perfidious woman, to so disregard your pride.
Age was dreaded then by both Trojan and Greek,
preferring to die young and beautiful on the battlefield.
She knew that.

Fall 1991

On Rodin's *The Helmet-Maker's Wife*
Liberty Winter

Her head bent in the same shame
she'd felt that first afternoon
when the Helmet Maker
brought her home.
Her tears fell as she set the table;
he pretended not to notice, just
blew a rose petal from her hair.

He showed her that night
how the poppies blow in sunlight,
how the dark waves unfurl.

After that he was afraid to lose her.

Fall 1991

On the Fifteenth Anniversary
Liberty Winter

See how these five small rooms expand, take shape
Pushing the four walls back to make a space
Where we may enter in and entertain ourselves.
Make music in our lives, speak French, observe
The stars, whate'er the wand of Ariel devises.
Coming by subway train, on foot, each with a
Charmed life, we take the caravan to Samarkand,
Tell fairy tales, then flirt with robber barons.
All hail our happy isle, these rooms to hire
"Burning in flames of pure and chaste desire."

HILR Fifteenth Anniversary program
April 1992

To Grayface

Liberty Winter

It's somewhat unnerving
the way Grayface flicks his tail.
Stretched out all sinews and muscles,
such extravagant hair! His long arms gray
but braceleted in black,
and all those softly padded toes.
Oh! he is the world to look upon
the way he slaps his tail upon the ground
lying out long and odalisque
his eyes round.

How bestial can you get
with Grayface the cat,
plunging your fingers through his hair
to where his skeleton is delicate.

Spring 1992

Armies of the Night

Liberty Winter

If what the U.S. is doing in Vietnam is right,
what is left to be called wrong?
                                    —William Sloane Coffin

Rolling back through the night in the bus, my cheek
against the cool window, listening to the sing-song
turn of the heavy wheels on the pavement:
It feels good to be good to be one with these good people.
The huge bus returning from storming the Pentagon
dark, but for one tiny bulb on the door of the john,
when suddenly a Roman thought struck me:
What if this war should suddenly end?
Did I need all this dying to feel good?

Would I feel grievously deprived if hundreds
of thousands of Americans stopped killing
and being killed by thousands of thousands of Vietnamese?
Must I have children blinded, their legs ripped off,
their country made a wasteland by our napalm
to know where morally I stand?
Who is the bully? The flag of which I boast
I am ashamed, or I who counsel in good faith
young men how to avoid the draft,
yet need an Armageddon to vent my wrath?

Fall 1992

Elmira Bussey and Her Book of Poems
Among the Missing
Liberty Winter

Elmira Bussey, I remember her in class. Another
conscientious, part-time lay poet, picking on my poems
so energetically the teacher had to defend them.
An elderly lady, petite, shoulders rounded a little,
curly hair, wrinkles in her face, but with two high pink
cheekbones, red lips, that when she smiled,
and she smiled often, glistened.
I remember her well, sitting at the head of the long table
by the teacher, questioning the propriety of my verse.

This flashback comes because I have *Among the Missing*
in my hand, and am wondering, can I toss it
just like that, this gentle volume of verse,
posthumously printed by the teacher and the members of the class?
Sorting out my crowded shelves just now
I picked this slender book to be among the first to go.
She's had, can I say, her day . . .
Oh, heavens no!

Fall 1993

Walker Street, Cambridge
Liberty Winter

I grant this is not quite a city. These trees,
their curled-up leaves in spring uncurling,
the violets jumping fences yard to yard,
and every morning starting with a song.
To me the most magnificent is the crow
way up atop the high-rise that I vowed
each night I'd tear down glass by brick,
watching and cursing the builders building it.
My neighbor's peach tree germinated from a stone.
I watch it blossom from my bedroom window and see
the tiniest, rounded fruit appear on every stem.
I take my laughter with the squirrels.
And up and down the street on every stoop
a cat sits, proud, possessive and secure.

Spring 1994

The Confession
Liberty Winter

I'd decided to make a confession
to my mother's minister.
He'd liked, enjoyed, admired Mother.
They read Plato together, and I got a kick
out of him myself,

so partly to get his goat, to perplex him
rather, I confessed to him.
"I knew I would benefit from my mother's death."
We had just entered her rose garden,
the minister and I,
on our way to the front of the house
where we would lie out in the sun
on lawn chairs, drink tea, and watch the polo ponies.

"All children do," he said, patting my grandfather's
gold pocket watch she had left him,
"that's natural." He had missed my point.
I pursued it. "Ah! but I knew I would ahead of time,"
loading my guilt on him,
which I could feel him drop like a hot stone.

Fall 1994

A Visit to the Hospital
Liberty Winter

You see I've made it to that place
we sometimes talked of, tearing
along the highways in the darkness,
lying in bed, my hand upon your breast
coitus interruptus. For that I now apologize.
Sweet idiot, you should have said
"You Catholic fake get off it."

It's worse than I'd imagined
who once was beautiful to women,
beautiful to myself as well, swinging
that tennis racquet through the air—one perfect motion—
I always felt beautiful when I heard you laugh.

Look at me if you can without disgust
and tell me that you love me still
for we are told that we are more than
flesh and blood. Should I rise now
I know my bones won't hold me.

Memento mori, I learned that as a kid.
It hung above my crib watching my fingers
steal ever so gently across my flesh
while wondering if I'd live to be a man.

Now when you lift my hand off this white sheet
and guide it to your lips, I hold my breath.
It is fearful what time is doing to me.
I don't dare look at my watch.

Spring 1995

Ani-Dove and the End of Rent Control
Liberty Winter

Ani-Dove, my slim-boned yellow cat,
wants to stay on Walker Terrace forever.
He loves the rusty, round black tabletop,
the fence he walks along gingerly
step by tiny step, and on the other side
their new and different gardens.
Then there's the sociability of the place.
It's taken him years of complicated finesse
to build up his cat friends. And there's
the enemy—the huge Angora, three houses down,
the oldest cat on the block
who comes on periodic visits.

Fall 1995

On Reading Milton's *Paradise Lost*
Liberty Winter

Mother, I can't but feel you're with me here,
sitting across the fireplace in your blue chair
while I read aloud (you being blind now)
how that Avenger fell, down—down
into Adamantine chains and wintry hoar
yet kept his pride. You laughed, liking that.
Your laugh, half-hearty, half a giggle.
I hear you now, see your shawl-covered shoulders lift.
You were a mixture all your life, half-fixed, half-free.

And how we laughed, so tickled both of us,
to read when our progenitor, heroic-built, though of terrestrial mold,
was led on by his doting wife, doting on him,
and on that inventive snake, not in submission crawling,
but head held high, in sidelong steps as he approached her.
You found the body of gentle Eve "delicious," pursing your lips,
pronouncing the word, just as you praised some special
dessert the waitress passed around your dining-room table,
say, a prune soufflé, or an apple tapioca pudding.

Fall 1995

From a Retired Actor to a Young Boy
Liberty Winter

Dear Friend, I'm putting this in a letter
asking you to tell my public I have not retired.
Inform them at my final curtain
they paid tribute to an actor
before he had begun developing his art.

The one they knew! Why he was just a clown
catching and throwing cues of little matter,
existing only until the curtain is down.
How thin the theater all seems now,
we actors but the shadows of our parts.

Here in my room I write, direct, and cast.
I put on Falstaff, I'm a baritone.
I dance to Salome.
This art of mine it knows no sex, nor age, nor time.
All's jumbled up, the way it is in fact.

If you remember me, that time we met,
or even if you don't, I want partic-
ularly to let you know. I cast you also,
please forgive me, you play
so many of my favorite parts.

Spring 1996

At Edgewood
Dorothy Weeden (1907-1978)
Liberty Winter

Like pinpoints of sun on water
her legs in elegant shoes
looked somehow borrowed.
Her laugh, she could have caught it
from a single lark today,
for in the hills it rang
a gathering cry. She used to say
her eyes could not seduce, they were too small,
pig eyes, she called them, those light soft blue.

Funny the water light dancing
and a sweeping phrase of codas
blowing by the bank
while sheltered from the wind
I sit where we last picked
bunches of marigolds for all her friends.
Funny, she could say an unkind thing
and make it kindly, and hate almost with love.

I think she'd be tickled pink
(her nose did wrinkle when she laughed,
her eyes grew smaller)
to think a silly friend of hers
was sitting by her Boone Lake water
listening to a bird and the scratching
of dry grass between the rock.
I swear it is not true your tomb is dark.

Fall 1996

120

A Rich Man Gave Me the Sky

Liberty Winter

In his ninety-third year
he stood straight and lean
by the water's edge
and with clear, pale eyes
looked up. "Clouds are my
favorite things,
especially cumulus."
I returned home in the ferry
and never saw him again.

I imagined for years following
all the places I might have visited
from the Barents Sea to the Sea
of Arafura, had he taken his pen
and written my name somewhere
between The University and The Church.

I used to think all I need do
is dig him up, push off the soil,
wake him and say, "We were such friends!"
But I loved the sky for the first time,
and learned like him
to watch the clouds change.

I am forgetting now to look.
I am letting my inheritance
slide through my fingers.

Spring 1997

Waiting

Nancy Lawder Wolcott

We are waiting
in still another public place,
a sterile space of S-shaped chairs
and steel tables littered
with tattered covers on crime
and scandals of the Royal Family.

We are waiting
as we have waited in other rooms
on other days, on other floors
with others, pale and patient,
hushed around us
(whispering, watching, wondering)

waiting for the time
when there will be
no more waiting . . .

On the darkest day of deep December,
in this drab, windowless room
I close my eyes to see
more light. And I listen
for footsteps,
the footsteps of an angel.

We are waiting—

Fall 1994

All Done

Nancy Lawder Wolcott

Everything was decided and divided
and done. Just like that.
That's all it was. It didn't even hurt.
Like a trip to the dentist
over fast—not so bad as dreaded.

There was still some numbness but underneath
a stone was moving off my heart and
I felt lighter and a little dizzy
at the loneness of me.

I stepped into our Volvo and closed the door.
From the curb he bent down
and kissed me. . . . Then
I rolled up the window and drove away.

Spring 1995

A Capital Self
Ruth Wolf

In Sight
and Sound
   of the Surging Sea
MySelf is longing to
   Soar with Thee!
BirdS Soaring over
Surging Surf
   TopS of treeS
Swaying in wind.
   If I had wingS
I'd ride on the topS—
   but rather alight
on a wave
   be carried up
     over
   then Swoop
down
   to the bottom
     UP
      over the top!

   Beyond the breakerS
I couldn't Stay
   but float into Shore
SmaShing my heart
   on rockS
or abandoned on Sand
   without Support
or direction
   for the journey.
Better to Stay
   on the Shore
in the firSt place

UnleSS your craft
iS So Strong
it will Support you
without
and within
wherever you go
on land
or on water.

I won't mind loSing
my place on earth.
I never did really
find it.
It'S loneSome
for me
Since I once had
you here;
Not loSt my way
never found it.
Except with you
can't do it alone.
The Sea beckonS me
aS if it were home
Where I belong
all along.

Roaring iS welcome
aS well aS water.
Wind will carry me
over the waveS,
Spraying foam
on the way,
Scattering dropS
around me.

Spring 1989

A Walk with Robert Frost

Frank Yaffee

On a Vermont autumn trip I dassn't fail
To tread on foot the Robert Frost Trail.
As I commenced my walk, I sensed by my side
A presence enormous. "Robert Frost!" I cried.
"Good Friend," the poet said, "allow me to guide you.
Permit me the pleasure of walking beside you."
He pointed to blueberry bushes emptied, graying,
And ferns yet green, though edges brittle, fraying,
To the hills in the distance awakening in the midmorn haze,
Their trees, shrubs streaked yellow in Autumn's dying days.
And he touched the bark lovingly of an old maple tree;
He had tapped its bark off, the sap oozing free.
The silver-white birches stood silently on guard,
Branches snarled, nigh naked, bowing in deference to the bard.
He read loud of his poetry posted some here and some there.
Oh! The joy of listening! The occasion so rare.
We sat on a stone bench deep in our walk.
He reminisced of the past. Oh! Such sweet talk!
When e'er he felt fearful, fretful, and worn,
Frost came back to God's Country, his vigor reborn.
We crossed a wee bridge, there 'neath—a wee brook.
He pondered the scene, his smile at the crook.
Here in summer's heat, he'd bathed his bare feet.
And at times alone, e'en his bare seat.
He laughed at the memories pictured in thought.
As I peered at his face of such character wrought.
We continued our journey, oblivious of time,
Frost declaiming his poetry with most exquisite of rhyme.
"Come back in the spring," he then said, "with my wild flowers
in full bloom.
They'll delight, exhilarate you, dispel all your gloom."
When we reached the end of this most memorable walk,
I turned to my host, but met with sheer shock.
For the venerable bard was no longer there!
He was with me, beside me, 'pon my oath I do swear!

I did walk with Robert Frost on the Robert Frost Trail.
Of this I'll not recant, my memories shan't fail.

Spring 1987

Green

Geraldine Zetzel

That spring, Lina the cook made Italy
into a new map for us—all green—
as the crop of fresh peas slowly
crept northwards to Florence.

"These are from south of Rome," she'd say.
The next week—"from the Marches."
Then "from Umbria"—then "Tuscany."
We felt them rising, urgent as a flood.

Each day at supper, the new peas soloed
on our plates—tiny globes
dressed with flecks of rosy ham,
ambrosial to our tongues.

At last—late May—Lina sailed
into the dining room, platter held high
in triumph over her head: "Piselli nostri!"
she announced, "Peas of our own!"

We bowed over our plates, we tasted.
Was anything ever so good?
The children hushed, dipping their spoons.
For ten days we revelled.

Then the season was over. The tide
gone on to Bologna, Milano, Turin—who knows?
flowing greenly up into
the passes, the Alps.
In Florence, it was time for morels.

Fall 1995